P9-DCZ-691

YOUNG PEOPLE'S STORY OF

OUR HERITAGE

CENTRAL

YOUNG PEOPLE'S
STORY OF
OUR HERITAGE

ARCHITECTURE

by

V. M. HILLYER and E. G. HUEY

New Edition Designed and Revised by Childrens Press, Chicago

Consultants

Howard Dearstyne, Associate Professor of Architecture
Illinois Institute of Technology, Chicago, Illinois

H.F. Koeper, Associate Professor of Architecture
University of Illinois, Chicago Circle Campus, Chicago, Illinois

Meredith Press, New York

Illustrations in the order in which they appear

UN Secretariat Building/2
Marina City on the Chicago River/4
Detail of Carson, Pirie, Scott & Company Ornamentation/9
Barrel Vault/13
Pointed Arch/13
Ribbed Arch/13
Flying Buttresses/13
Towers of Notre Dame/14
Flying Buttresses of Notre Dame/15
St. Chapelle/16
Diagram of Latin Cross Cathedral/17
Rheims Cathedral/18
Durham Cathedral/22
Salisbury Cathedral/23
Lincoln Cathedral/24
Westminster Abbey/25
Canterbury Cathedral/25
Cologne Cathedral/26
Town Hall, Antwerp/27
Grand Place, Brussels/28
Burgos Cathedral/30
The Doge's Palace/33
The Blue Mosque/34
The Alhambra/36
A Minaret/37
A Mosque in Cordova/38
Court of the Lions, Alhambra/38
Giralda Tower/40
The Taj Mahal/41
Il Duomo, Florence/44
Riccardi Palace/46
St. Peter's/48
Plan of St. Peter's/50
Haddon Hall/53
The Rows/54
Shakespeare's Birthplace/54
Chateau Blois/57
Stairway of the Chateau Blois/58
Chateau Chambord/60
Chateau Fontainebleau/62
The Louvre and Tuileries/62
Chateau Versailles/64
Hall of Mirrors, Versailles/64
Hôtel des Invalides/66
The French Panthéon/67
Santa Maria della Salute/69
Cathedral in Mexico City/71
Banqueting Hall, Whitehall/73
St. Paul's Cathedral/74
Christopher Wren Church/75
Lincoln's Log-Cabin Birthplace/77
St. Luke's Church/77
Independence Hall/80
Mt. Vernon/80
University of Virginia/80
Washington Monument/81
Mission at Carmel/83
The White House/84
The Capitol, Washington, D.C./84
Statue of Abraham Lincoln, Lincoln Memorial/88
Lincoln Memorial/89
A Simple Beam Bridge/90
The Landwasser Viaduct/90
Crown Point Bridge/90
Chicago Skyway Toll Bridge/90
Brooklyn Bridge/91
Pont du Gard/92
Salginatobel Bridge/93
Chesapeake Bay Bridge/95
New York Skyscrapers and the Statue of Liberty/96
Empire State Building/97
Guaranty Building/99
Auditorium Theater Building/100
Carson, Pirie, Scott & Company Building/100
Taliesin West/102
Kaufman Residence/102
Diagram of Core and Cantilever Building/104
Marina City/105
Johnson Wax Tower/105
Guggenheim Museum/105
Fagus Works/106
The Bauhaus/107
Barcelona Pavilion/108
Seagram Building/110
860-880-900-910 N. Lake Shore Drive Apartments/110
Apartment Building in Marseilles/112
Chapel at Ronchamp/112
Lincoln Center/115
Lever House/116
John Hancock Center/116
Inland Steel Company Building/117
St. Paul's Lutheran Church/118
Air Force Academy Cadet Chapel/118
Roma-Palazzetto dello Sport/120
The Hippodrome/120
University of Mexico Library/121
Chicago Circle Campus/122
TWA Terminal Building/122
Old Orchard Shopping Center/122

Library of Congress Catalog Card Number: 66-11327

Contents

Acknowledgments / 8

Gothic Architecture—
Pointing toward Heaven / 10

French Gothic Cathedrals / 14

English Country Cathedrals / 20

Gothic Architecture
Elsewhere in Europe / 27

Mohammedan Buildings / 35

Renaissance Architecture / 42

The Italian Renaissance / 47

English Tudor Architecture / 52

French Renaissance Architecture / 56

Baroque Architecture / 68

English Renaissance Architecture / 72

Architecture in America / 76

Washington, D.C. / 85

Bridges of the World—
Yesterday and Today / 91

Scrapers of the Sky / 97

Frank Lloyd Wright / 103

Steel and Glass—
Walter Gropius and Mies van der Rohe / 106

Sculptured Concrete—
Le Corbusier / 111

Architecture Today / 114

Index to Architecture,
Gothic—Modern / 124

Credits / 127

Acknowledgments

Cover drawing: John Hollis

Cover photograph: Farnsworth House, Plano, Illinois; Mies van der Rohe, architect.
Hedrich-Blessing Photograph

Page 2: A view of the United Nations Secretariat Building on the East River, New York.
American Airlines

Frontis: Aerial view of the Chicago River looking west toward Marina City.
American Airlines

Opposite: Detail of the ornamentation of the Carson, Pirie, Scott & Company Building, Chicago; Louis Sullivan, architect.
Hedrich-Blessing Photograph

Designed by John Hollis

Edited by Joan Downing

ARCHITECTURE

Gothic—Modern

Gothic Architecture—Pointing toward Heaven

Now I'm going to tell you about a kind of architecture named for some people who did not have an architecture of their own. Huts were the only things they ever built. Yet the kind of architecture named for these people is one of the most important in the world.

That certainly seems strange, doesn't it?

The people who didn't know how to build anything but huts were the Goths. The beautiful architecture that the Goths didn't have anything to do with is called Gothic architecture. Why is it called Gothic architecture if the Goths didn't have anything to do with it?

The reason is a strange one. Most people today think that Gothic architecture is very wonderful, and that Gothic buildings are very beautiful. But there were people who despised these beautiful buildings. They thought any architecture that didn't come from Greece or Rome was no good. They thought it was crude and rough and uncivilized. The crudest, roughest, and most uncivilized people they could think of were the Goths who had conquered Rome, so they called this beautiful architecture Gothic, not only to show how crude they thought it was, but because they thought the Goths had begun it.

Gothic architecture grew out of Romanesque architecture. The builders kept trying to make stone ceilings over the naves of the churches because stone was safer from fire than wood was. At first the stone ceiling was a barrel vault, shaped like the side of a barrel. The barrel vault took a great deal of wooden centering to build, because the vault was quite long and each part had to be held up by the centering until all the stones were in place. The centering took so much wood that it was a wonderful thing when someone found a way of building vaults with very little centering. Two curved ribs like arches or parts of hoops that crossed in the middle of the vault were built first and then the rest of the vault could be put in a little at a time.

Then another discovery was made. This was that a pointed arch sometimes was better than a round arch. It wasn't really a new discovery, for the people in Asia Minor had used pointed arches for many years. The knights brought the idea back to Europe when they returned from their Crusades in the Holy Land. You might not think that such a little thing as making an arch pointed on top instead of round would be important. But important it was, and this is why.

A round arch has to be just as high as it is wide. The wider the opening it has to cover, the higher the round arch has to be. But a pointed arch is different. You can build a pointed arch as high or as low as you want, no matter how wide the opening is that it has to stretch across. If you will put your fingertips together so they form an arch you can understand the reason for this. If you keep your hands the same distance apart you can only form one round arch with your fingers. But you can form pointed arches of several different sizes by curving your fingers and keeping your hands still.

The builders of the stone cathedrals found it much easier to build vaults over a wide nave or aisle by using pointed arches instead of round arches.

Of course these stone vaults pushed down on the walls and also pushed sideways. So the walls had to be very thick and very well braced with buttresses. But the builders found that when they used ribbed vaults instead of plain barrel vaults, most of the side push came just at the ends of the ribs. They found that if they put heavy buttresses at the ends of the ribs, the rest of the wall could be made very thin. The walls between the buttresses finally became so unnecessary for holding up the roof that they were made of glass. The walls became walls of glass between buttresses of stone.

Not only did the walls get lighter, but a new kind of buttress—the *flying buttress*—was designed. A flying buttress is one that leans against the wall like a prop. Flying buttresses press against the top of the walls and keep the walls from being pushed over by the weight of the vault and the roof.

These three innovations—the ribbed vault, the glass walls between buttresses, and flying buttresses—are the three most important things to remember, for they made possible that beautiful kind of architecture known as Gothic.

Gothic architecture was as different from the Greek and Roman as it could be. The Greek and Roman buildings were solidly set on the ground. Almost all the weight pushed straight down. But a Gothic cathedral was a balance of all sorts of thrusts and pushes and forces. Where there was a side push, there was a buttress to push against it.

In the Greek and Roman temples most of the lines ran lengthwise. They were horizontal buildings. The Gothic cathedrals climbed into the air as though reaching up toward heaven. The lines seem to carry the eye upward from the ground.

Barrel Vault

Pointed Arch

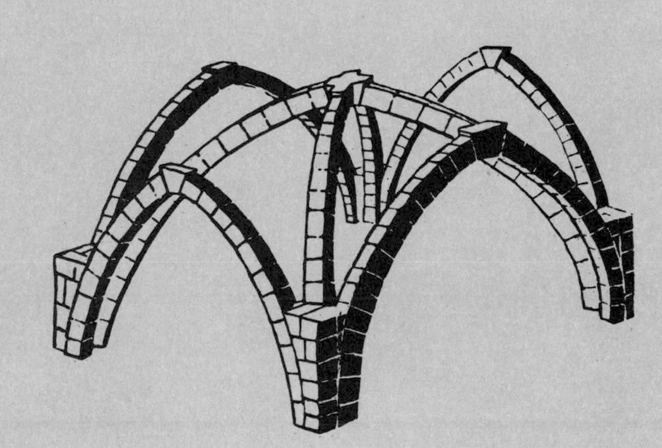

Ribbed Arch

Flying Buttresses

French Gothic Cathedrals

Today big buildings take only months to build. It often took hundreds of years to build big Gothic buildings. It took more than six hundred years to build one Gothic building, Cologne Cathedral.

The most important Gothic buildings were the cathedrals. When "Gothic" is mentioned, most people think of France, for France has some of the finest Gothic cathedrals in the world.

The Gothic cathedrals were built with loving care. Everyone in the village and the surrounding country did his bit for the cathedral. The stones were shaped and set in place by the members of the guilds, which were clubs of workmen. The guild would not let any work pass that was not good work. There was nothing "fake" about a cathedral. The stone carvings high up in the roof were just as carefully made as they would have been if people could get near enough to examine them.

View of the towers at the west end of Notre Dame Cathedral, Paris

Perhaps this is why the Gothic cathedrals rate next to the Greek buildings as the world's most wonderful examples of architecture. The men who built the Greek temples and the men who built the Gothic cathedrals left behind them very different kinds of architecture. But they were alike in the honesty of their work.

Most of the French Gothic cathedrals were built to the glory of Mary, the mother of Christ, who in French was called Notre Dame—Our Lady. There were so many cathedrals of Notre Dame built that we generally call the cathedral simply by the name of the town it is in, such as Chartres or Rheims. But if anyone speaks of just the Cathedral of Notre Dame, he usually means Notre Dame of Paris.

Notre Dame of Paris has on the west end—the end opposite the altar—two large towers. Beneath the towers and in the center are the doorways, one to the nave and one

opposite: Flying buttresses of the Cathedral of Notre Dame, Paris

French Embassy Press and Information Division, New York

Stained glass windows of St. Chapelle, Paris

to each side aisle. The doorways are covered with rows of statues of prophets and saints, the head of one statue below the feet of another. Above each doorway is a row of very large statues of kings. Above the kings is a huge round window called a *wheel window* or *rose window*. The rose window is filled with brilliant colored pieces of glass—*stained glass*—that cast a soft purplish glow inside the church.

This cathedral in Paris is in the form of a Latin cross, as are nearly all the Gothic churches. The arms of the cross are called the *transepts* of the cathedral. The place where the transepts cross the nave is called the *crossing*. Over the crossing was built a tall slender spire. You can see this spire between the towers in the picture.

The front of a building is called the façade (fas-sahd). Façade means about the same thing as face. Notre Dame of Paris is said to have the finest façade of any Gothic cathedral in the world. In fact, each of the great cathedrals of France has some part that is considered the best in the world. What a building it would make if the best of each cathedral were put together to make one best cathedral! But perhaps such a building wouldn't be as interesting, after all, as the separate cathedrals.

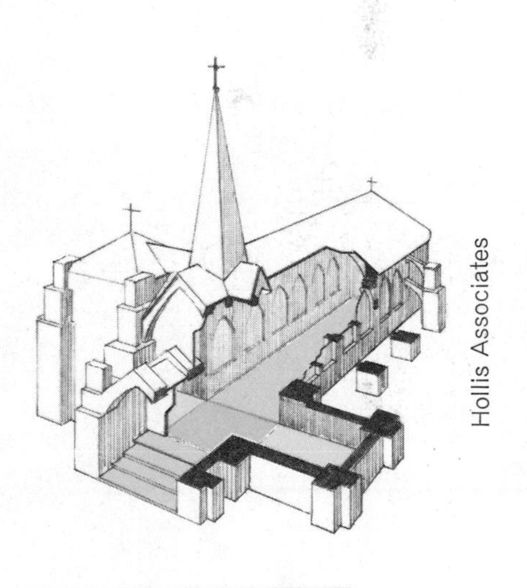
Hollis Associates

Diagram of a Latin Cross type of Gothic Cathedral

The towers with square tops on the cathedral of Paris were meant to have tall spires on them. But by the time the cathedral was ready for the spires, so many years had gone by that the spires were never built. On some cathedrals one tower was built and the other never finished. On one very fine cathedral the spires were put on at different times, so that they are not alike. This is the famous Cathedral of Chartres.

Chartres is a little city about sixty miles from Paris. The Cathedral of Chartres is noted not only for its two spires but for the wonderful stained glass windows in its walls. You remember that Gothic churches had walls of glass. This glass was made in brilliant color to show scenes from Bible stories. The sunlight streaming through the colored glass has a marvelously beautiful effect on the interior. Instead of the glass of Chartres Cathedral, however, the illustration in our book is a picture of the interior of a church in Paris called the Sainte Chapelle. Notice how much of the wall space is glass. The stone parts, as you can see, are hardly more than a framework for whole walls of glass.

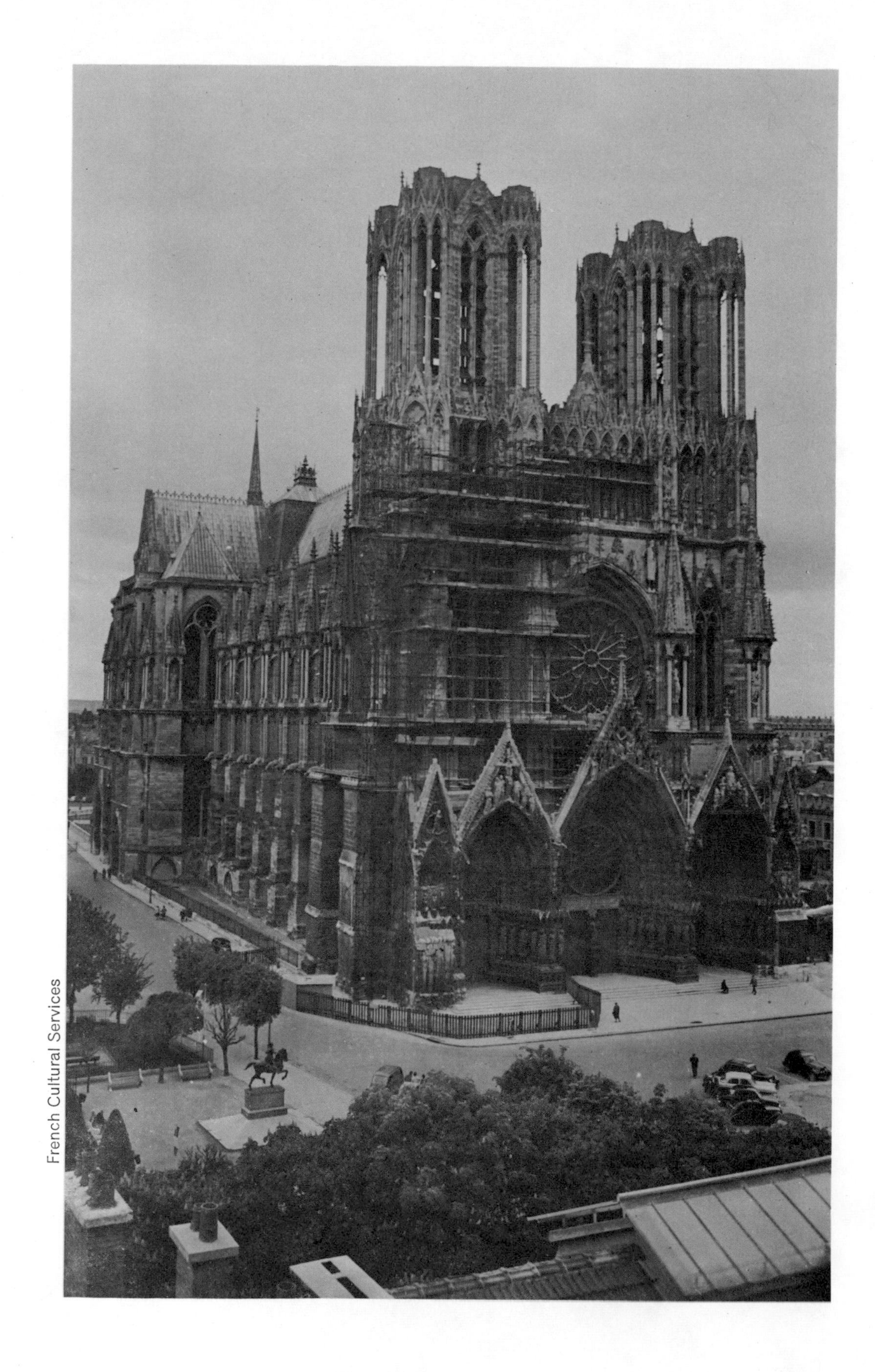

French Cultural Services

The glass was held by stone framework in the windows, and the separate pieces of glass were kept in place with strips of lead. The stone framework holding the glass in the windows is called *tracery*.

As new Gothic cathedrals were built, the tracery was made in different shapes. Often the shape of the tracery is a good way to tell in what period the cathedral was built.

Rheims Cathedral is thought to have the best *portals*, or doorways. It is famous also for its proportion, or shape as a whole building. And many of the carved stone statues that are all over the building are famous. Unfortunately this beautiful cathedral was in the fighting area during World War I and the German shells that struck it damaged it terribly. After the war the damage was repaired as carefully as possible, so that Rheims looks almost the same as before.

Fortunately this cathedral could be repaired, but many of the beautiful buildings of the past have been destroyed in wars or so badly damaged that they could not be repaired. The Parthenon was blown up by an explosion during a war.

The best Gothic nave is thought by many to be the nave of the cathedral at Amiens.

Let's see what the best things are from the cathedrals we have mentioned: The façade of Notre Dame of Paris, the spires and glass of Chartres, the doorways of Rheims, the statues of Rheims, and the nave of Amiens.

Northern France has many Gothic buildings. Almost every town has its Gothic church or cathedral. The cathedrals were built to the glory of God and all the people added what they could to the glory of the church. All the art of the Middle Ages was found there. Paintings and stained glass, sculpture and architecture, music and tapestry, jewels and precious metals for the altar—all were part of these great buildings or of the religious services held in them.

Rheims Cathedral, France

English Country Cathedrals

Almost all the French Gothic cathedrals are in cities or towns. They have very little open ground around them. Dwelling houses and shops are crowded so closely about them that it is often hard to get a good view of the outside of a French cathedral.

English Gothic cathedrals are just the opposite. They were generally built out in the country, so most of the English cathedrals have plenty of open space around them—lawns and trees instead of stores and crowded streets. They stand in beautiful settings which make the buildings themselves look even more beautiful.

Now why should cathedrals be in the cities in France and in the country in England?

In France the cathedrals were built by the people of the towns. They were used much more often than a church is used now. The French cathedrals were the schools, the theaters, the public meeting places of the people, besides being houses for prayer and worship. They had to be in the center of things, because they were so important in the lives of the people of the towns.

But in England the cathedrals were usually built by the monks for their own use. The village people had parish churches where they could worship. Of course ordinary people could worship in the cathedrals, but the cathedrals were built chiefly for the monks. Because monasteries were places where the monks could get away from the world outside, they were more often built in the country away from the cities. And of course the monastery or abbey church was built in the country, too.

That is one difference between English Gothic and French Gothic—one is usually in the country, the other in the city.

Another difference is that English cathedrals are much longer for their width than French cathedrals are. An English cathedral looks long and narrow, while a French cathedral looks short and wide. The eastern ends of the English cathedral where the monks worshiped had to be much longer because there were so many monks. The French cathedrals with their crowds of people who came to listen to their priest, needed a wider and shorter space so all the people could hear him. Each country shaped its cathedrals to fit the use to which the cathedrals were put.

Here is another difference.

Most of the French cathedrals have doors at their western ends opening into the nave and aisles. Most of the English cathedrals have doors at the side, besides those at the end, with little porches to keep out the wind and rain.

And here is yet another difference.

Most of the French Gothic cathedrals have two towers on their western ends above the doors. But many of the English Gothic cathedrals have their main tower over the crossing of the transept and nave, and sometimes there are no towers at all on the western end.

So you can see again that the same kind of architecture is different in different countries.

An important thing to remember about Gothic cathedrals is that few cathedrals were completed during the period in which they were started. In many cases a cathedral was begun as a Romanesque building and finished as a Gothic building, years later. The great Durham Cathedral, which was built in England as a fort against the Scots as well as a church, has a Norman nave but Gothic towers.

Historical Pictures Service, Chicago

above: Durham Cathedral, England

opposite: Salisbury Cathedral, England

Durham is plainer, less decorated on the outside, than other cathedrals and for this reason it looks strong and solid and very dignified.

As time went on, the Gothic style changed in England. There are really four kinds of Gothic there, corresponding to four different periods of time. Sometimes it took so long to build a cathedral that all four periods of architecture can be found in one building.

In the thirteenth century churches were built in *Early English* Gothic. Salisbury Cathedral, which has the tallest spire in England, is Early English.

British Travel Association Photo

Historical Pictures Service, Chicago

Lincoln Cathedral, England

In the fourteenth century the style was *Decorated* Gothic. The nave and east end of Lincoln Cathedral is in the Decorated style.

In the fifteenth century the style was *Perpendicular* Gothic. Perpendicular is a word meaning straight up and down. The towers of Canterbury Cathedral are Perpendicular Gothic.

And last came the *Tudor* period. The famous chapel of Henry VII in Westminster Abbey is Tudor.

Westminster Abbey itself is more like French cathedrals than most English buildings, perhaps partly because it is in a city—London. It is famous as the burial place of many of England's great men.

Two other famous cathedrals are Peterborough Cathedral, which has huge pointed archways over the doors—archways that are as high as the roof—and Wells cathedral, which has a famous tower over the crossing.

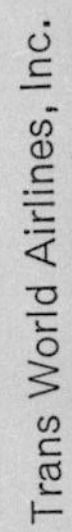

British Travel Association Photo

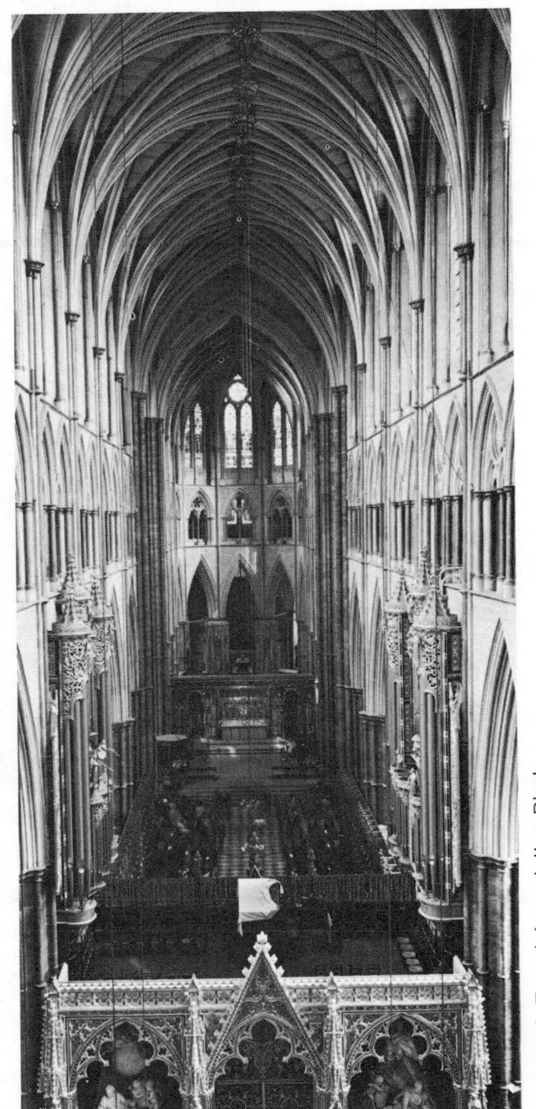

British Travel Association Photo

above: An interior view of Westminster Abbey, London

above left: An exterior view of Westminster Abbey, London

below left: Canterbury Cathedral, England

Trans World Airlines, Inc.

Gothic Architecture Elsewhere in Europe

Cologne, in Germany, is a big city famous for its huge Gothic cathedral. Cologne Cathedral is the largest Gothic church of northern Europe. The spires are five hundred feet high—as high as fifteen three-story houses.

Cologne Cathedral was begun in 1248 and wasn't finished until 1880, more than six hundred years later. But that was better than many cathedrals, which were not finished at all and probably never will be.

Cologne Cathedral is so wide for its length that to many people it doesn't seem as beautiful as the French cathedrals. Its twin western towers with their tall spires are so big and bulky at the bottom that they make the rest of the building look smaller than it is. The proportions of one part of the building compared with another are not as fine as they might be. This means that the building doesn't look just right as a whole, although each part by itself may be correctly and splendidly made. It is easy to forget the cathedral's imperfections when you see the thousands of carved stone figures, the pinnacles, towers, and flying buttresses that make this building one of the best known in the world. It is magnificent, huge, impressive.

In Antwerp is the most impressive church in Belgium—Antwerp Cathedral. This cathedral has a place for two towers on its western front, but only one tower is there. The other one was never built. Where it might have been there is just a little steeple.

The one big tower rises high in the air and becomes narrower at the top, like a spire. It has so much stone carving on it that it looks like lacework made of stone. The

left: Cologne Cathedral, Germany

right: Town Hall, Antwerp, Belgium

Official Belgian Tourist Bureau, New York

tower is graceful, but the lacy look seems a little too fancy. Probably Antwerp Cathedral really looks better because it has only one tower.

This is just one of the many beautiful towers in Belgium. Many of them are not on churches at all but stand by themselves. They are often called singing towers because the bells inside ring out beautiful music. Singing towers were often useful as well as beautiful. The peal of the bells called the people together, spread an alarm in time of danger, and rang out in triumph to announce good news. Belgium can be proud of her beautiful Gothic towers.

Besides the singing towers there are many other Gothic buildings in Belgium that aren't churches. Gothic architecture suits churches well and the most beautiful Gothic buildings *are* churches, but many of the other Belgian Gothic buildings are beautiful too. Naturally, these buildings would not be shaped like a cross. Some of them have towers and spires like churches and some have not. Some were built by the towns for town halls where the public business was carried on. Some were built as clubhouses, or headquarters, for guilds. Each kind of trade or business had its own guild, or band of skilled workers. There were guilds of stonemasons, goldsmiths, ship captains, merchants, butchers, bakers, and candlestick makers. Of course each guild wanted its own clubhouse, or guildhall. Many Belgian guildhalls show very beautiful Gothic architecture.

Many of the Gothic town halls and guildhalls had steep roofs with rows of dormer windows. A dormer window is the kind that is built in a sloping roof. The Cloth Hall at Ypres was one of the most famous Belgian buildings of the Middle Ages, but it was burned down during World War I.

Grand Place, the Town Hall in Brussels, Belgium

Official Belgian Tourist Bureau, New York

Spanish National Tourist Office, Chicago

Spanish National Tourist Office, Chicago

Spanish National Tourist Office, Chicago

One of the largest Gothic cathedrals in the world is in Spain. It is in the little Spanish town of Burgos. The twin towers with their tall spires remind one a little of the towers of Cologne. There is a big eight-sided tower in the middle, besides the two spires at the end. Around the cathedral at Burgos are cloisters, chapels, and an archbishop's palace.

Burgos is in the northern part of Spain and is more like French and German cathedrals than the Spanish churches farther south. The Moors from Arabia had long ruled the south of Spain and the Gothic cathedrals there have many details that were suggested to the Spanish builders by the Moorish buildings.

opposite left: The towers of Burgos Cathedral, Spain

opposite right: Interior view of Burgos Cathedral, Spain

opposite center: The façade of Burgos Cathedral, Spain

below left: Panoramic view of Burgos showing the Cathedral spires

Spanish National Tourist Office, Chicago

Now for a quick trip across the Pyrenees, across France, across the Alps to Italy to see the Gothic buildings of Venice.

On the square of St. Mark stands the Cathedral of St. Mark with its five domes and Byzantine architecture. Next to St. Mark's on the square stands a long building four stories high. It is called the Doge's Palace. The Doge was the duke and ruler of Venice. The palace of the doges is Gothic (notice the pointed arches), but it is quite different from all other Gothic buildings. The two lower stories have long rows of the pointed arches on columns. Rows of arches like these, you remember, are called arcades. The arcades form covered porches around the Doge's Palace.

The upper hall of the Doge's Palace has flat walls of pink and white marble in a pattern. The flat upper half of the walls makes the fancier lower half look better. If more of the Doge's Palace was like the upper part it would be too plain. As it is, the whole building makes a beautiful part of the beautiful square of St. Mark.

Other smaller palaces and houses in the Gothic style can be found in Venice. You have to take a boat to see them, for most of them are on canals. A boat called a gondola can take you right up to the water steps leading to the front door.

The Doge's Palace, Venice

Photograph by Ente Provinciale per il Turismo—Venice

Turkish Tourism and Information Office, New York

The Mosque of Sultan Ahmed I, Istanbul (The Blue Mosque)

Mohammedan Buildings

Ali Baba came to the cave of the forty thieves. The door in the rock was shut. "Open sesame," said Ali Baba, and the door swung open.

Ali Baba was a Mohammedan. So was Sinbad the Sailor, so were Prince Agib and all the rest of those fascinating people who appear in *The Arabian Nights.*

"Open sesame." Let's see if the magic words will open the door of this chapter to show the treasures of Mohammedan architecture.

The Mohammedans believe in a book called the Koran, which is for them what the Bible is for Christians. Now, the Koran forbade any Mohammedan to make a picture or a likeness of any living thing. So you can guess that a Mohammedan temple, or *mosque* as it is called, must be very different from a Gothic cathedral, which is covered with hundreds of statues of men and animals and plants.

Another difference you would probably notice at once if you were in Istanbul or any other Mohammedan city would be the number of domes. These domes are not usually round, but shaped like half an egg or an onion and they often have points on the tops like the end of a fat turnip or beet. But all the mosques do not have domes, for a Mohammedan dome used to be the sign of a tomb and only in buildings that served as a tomb for someone was a dome built.

When you get close to a Mohammedan building you notice that the builders must have been good carvers of stone and marble. Their carving is a pattern of straight lines and curves, squares and circles, diamond shapes and star shapes, zigzags and crisscrosses. Some of the carving is so fine that it forms a network that looks like stone lace.

Historical Pictures Service, Chicago

above: Interior dome carving in the Hall of the Abencerrages, Alhambra, Granada

right: Arabesques of the Alhambra, Granada

opposite right: Minaret on the Mosque of d'Ibn Tonloun, Cairo

Spanish National Tourist Office, Chicago

Inside the buildings the carving and decorations are even richer than those outside the buildings. The designs are called *arabesques* because the first Mohammedans were Arabs and the Arabs built many mosques decorated in this way. Sometimes the arabesques are writings from the Koran. The Arabian letters are graceful and make beautiful decorations.

Inside these Mohammedan buildings we often find still another form of decoration that other buildings do not have. The vaults under the domes (the ceilings of the rooms) often have a curious carved work that looks like hundreds of little stone icicles hanging down from the roof.

In every Mohammedan village there is at least one *minaret,* or tower, for the *muezzin,* a man who climbs up five times a day to call the people to prayer. Some of the mosques have a minaret at each corner.

"Come to prayer, come to prayer. There is no god but Allah and Mohammed is his prophet," sings the muezzin, and then all good Mohammedans face toward the sacred city of Mecca and kneel in prayer. Mecca is the sacred city because Mohammed himself was born and lived there. Each Mohammedan mosque has a niche or hollow in the wall nearest Mecca. This niche takes the place of the altar in a church or temple.

The Mohammedan religion spread quickly from Arabia where it started, for the Arabs were great conquerors. Eastward it spread, farther and farther, through Persia and across India. Bagdad became the capital city of these eastern Mohammedans. Westward the Arabs pushed across Egypt, across northern Africa until they came to the Strait of Gibraltar. Even this did not stop them. They built boats and sailed across to Spain. Through Spain they spread until they got as far as France. All Europe would probably have become Mohammedan if the French had not stopped the Arabs in a battle fought at the town of Tours, in France.

Egyptian State Tourist Administration. Photo by Sobhi Afifi.

Historical Pictures Service, Chicago

Historical Pictures Service, Chicago

But much of Spain did become Mohammedan. The Arabs in Spain were called Moors. The Moors set up a capital at Cordova for all the western Mohammedans, just as Bagdad was the eastern capital, just as the Roman Empire had once had both an eastern and a western capital—Rome and Constantinople. For over seven hundred years the Moors ruled in Spain until they were finally driven out at about the time of Columbus.

In Cordova the Moors built a huge mosque which is still standing there. You remember how the Mohammedans turned the Christian church of St. Sophia in Constantinople into a mosque. In Cordova just the opposite happened. For when the Moors were finally driven out of Spain the Christians turned the Mohammedan mosque into a church. And it is still a church.

By far the most famous Mohammedan building in Spain is the Alhambra. The Alhambra was built by the Moorish kings of Granada in Spain as a kind of fortress palace. The Alhambra is on a tall hill of rock with steep cliffs that helped keep back enemies. Inside the different buildings were guard rooms and halls, gardens and courts, all decorated with thousands of arabesques. The Court of Lions is one part of the Alhambra that you may have heard of. It looks something like a cloister, for around its four sides are arcades. In the middle is a big marble basin, held on the backs of twelve lions, which is used as a fountain.

We don't know why the Moors carved marble lions, for they were not supposed to carve statues of living things. Maybe the lions were an exception that proved the rule. Maybe the lions were carved by Christians and captured and brought to the Alhambra by the Moors.

Another noted building in Spain left by the Moors is called the Giralda (Hee-ral'da) Tower. Giralda meant weather vane. The weather vane is on the very top of the tower. It is a figure of *Faith* that swings with the wind.

above left: Mosque in Cordova, Spain

below left: Court of the Lions, Alhambra, Granada

Spanish National Tourist Office, Chicago

The top three stories of the tower are Christian Renaissance architecture, because when the Christians finally drove the Moors out of Spain they used the Mohammedan buildings for their own needs and often added to them.

Now I'm going to take you from Spain in the West to India in the East. In Agra, India, lived a Mohammedan ruler who erected a tomb in honor of his wife.

This tomb is called the Taj Mahal. Because it was a tomb, it was crowned with a dome. Many travelers who have seen it have called it the most beautiful building in the world. The Taj Mahal is built all of marble and shines in the sun like a beautiful white jewel. Around the building are gardens, trees, lawns, and fountains and right in front of it is a long rectangular pool of water that reflects the trees and the Taj Mahal.

And with the Taj Mahal we will end our story of Mohammedan buildings.

left: Giralda Tower, Seville

above right: Taj Mahal, Agra, India

below right: Entrance to the gardens of the Taj Mahal, Agra

American President Lines

Trans World Airlines, Inc.

Renaissance Architecture

In the year 1296 a cathedral was being built in Florence, Italy. The cathedral was almost finished except for a huge dome on top. Then one day the workmen had to stop work and leave the cathedral unfinished. The architect had died and, as he was the only person who knew how to build a dome big enough for this cathedral, the cathedral remained unfinished for a long time. The architect had left no drawings or plans to guide the builders. He had told no one how he thought the dome should be built. So for over a hundred years the cathedral at Florence stood there with a big hole in the crossing where the dome ought to have been. Finally it was decided to hold a competition to see if anyone could be found who could build the dome and thus finish the cathedral.

In the competition many plans were suggested. One man said he was sure he could build the dome, but he would have to have a big column underneath the center to hold it up. Another man said he could build it, but he would have to have the help of a big pile of earth.

"If," said this one, "we mix gold coins with the earth and put this earth in a huge pile where the dome is to be, then we can build the dome around the pile. When the dome is completed, invite the people to carry off the earth to look for the coins. When all the earth is carried away, there will stand our dome."

The man who won the competition and got the job was named Brunelleschi (Brew-nel-less'kee). He had studied the old Roman buildings in Rome. He had worked as a sculptor, and he was a very good architect. Brunelleschi said he could build the dome, and build it without the wooden centering that would use up such a lot of timber. But in spite of Brunelleschi's confidence, the men in charge didn't feel quite so sure he could do what he said he could. So they made the sculptor Ghiberti (Gee-bear'tee) an architect for the dome, too.

Now, Ghiberti was a fine sculptor but he really hadn't any idea how to build the dome. He therefore did no work on it, although he was getting as much pay for the job as Brunelleschi, who did all the planning. Of course this didn't please Brunelleschi at all. So Brunelleschi pretended to be sick and stayed home in bed. Then the workmen had to stop work, for Ghiberti didn't know what to tell them to do next. So as long as Brunelleschi stayed in bed the work waited.

But in spite of this Ghiberti was not taken from the job, so Brunelleschi had to try another way of getting rid of him. He told the men in charge that he thought it best to divide the work between the two architects.

"There are two difficult things to be done," said Brunelleschi, "the bridges upon which the masons must stand and the chain which is to bind together the eight sides of the dome. Let Ghiberti take one of them, and I will take the other, that no more time be lost."

This did the trick. Ghiberti chose the chain, but couldn't make it work. He was soon taken off the job, and Brunelleschi was able to go ahead alone.

Brunelleschi finished the dome successfully. It is a different kind of dome from the dome of the Roman Pantheon, and it is different from the dome of St. Sophia. The dome is of brick and it has ribs of stone running down from the top. These ribs divide the dome into eight parts or sides, so it isn't smoothly round like most domes. For another thing, this dome has a little *cupola* or tiny tower on top known as a *lantern,* although there is no light burning inside.

Just how Brunelleschi managed to build the dome without using centering is a mystery. But he did build it—and built it well. Today it still rises above the roofs of Florence to be seen from far and near, one of the great domes of the world. It gives the cathedral its name, the Duomo. If you go to Florence you will see near the Duomo a statue of Brunelleschi. He is shown seated, looking up at the dome, with plans on his lap.

There is still another reason for telling you about Brunelleschi. He was the first architect of a new kind of architecture known as *Renaissance.*

The Renaissance was a rebirth of interest in life—in writing, painting, sculpture, and architecture. It was

especially a rebirth of interest in everything left by the ancient Greeks and Romans. I have told you that Brunelleschi studied the old Roman ruins. He had measured them, drawn pictures of them, and learned all he could about them. So when Brunelleschi designed buildings, he used the kinds of columns and decorations and vaults and plans that he admired from studying the Roman ruins. I don't mean he built copies of Roman buildings. He just used them to go by. And so did the Italian architects after Brunelleschi.

The Italians didn't care much for Gothic architecture. There was too much sunlight in Italy for churches with walls of glass. The Italians liked their buildings dark and cool inside, instead of full of sunlight, even if the sunlight did come through the marvelous stained glass windows of a Gothic cathedral.

This new Renaissance architecture was good in many ways, but in some ways it was not so good. The Gothic buildings had always been built so that every part of the building had its own special job to do. The buttresses were to push against the walls. The decorations carved on top of the buttresses were to give them more weight so they could hold more solidly. The stained glass windows and the statues were to tell Bible stories to people who couldn't read. There was scarcely any part of a Gothic building that was not honest or useful.

But the Renaissance buildings weren't always so honest. Often they were designed just to look good. Columns and pilasters were put on for decoration, without really helping to hold up anything, as columns should. An ornament should look like an ornament, not like a column, which should be a hard-working, load-bearing support.

Sometimes a Renaissance architect would cover a Gothic building with Renaissance ornament, to make it look like a Renaissance building.

But many of the Renaissance buildings were honest buildings. The best artists of the time became architects and designed buildings. New Gothic cathedrals were no longer built. Indeed, there were almost enough churches already, so most of the Renaissance buildings were palaces or government buildings or libraries.

Italian State Tourist Office-Enit. Foto Enit-Roma.

Brunelleschi's Dome, Il Duomo, Florence

Historical Pictures Service, Chicago

The Italian Renaissance

In 1492, as most of us know, Columbus discovered America. So it is easy to remember when Renaissance architecture began in Italy. It was in the same century as 1492, the fourteen-hundreds. Some of the earliest Renaissance buildings of the fourteen-hundreds are the best.

The Riccardi Palace in Florence looks more like a fort than a palace. Notice the iron bars on the lower windows and the heavy rough stones in the lower story. That kind of stonework is called *rusticated.* The stones bulge out from the joints between them. This makes the building look strong and solid.

The archways on the ground floor were built to open to the courtyard. The doors and windows with iron bars that show in the picture were filled in later.

The top of the building is crowned by a ledge that sticks out all around the wall. Such a ledge is called a *cornice.* The cornice finished off the top of a building just the way a capital finished off the top of a column. The windows have round arches, not pointed like Gothic arches.

The building is more like a palace inside than outside. In the middle of the inside is an open courtyard that has balconies around it. There is a big banquet hall, a library, and other finely furnished rooms. This Renaissance building is called the Riccardi Palace.

Now is a good time to notice a big difference between Gothic and Renaissance buildings. In Gothic buildings most of the lines are up and down. The eye is carried from the ground straight up to the top of the building. But in Renaissance buildings most of the lines are lengthwise—horizontal. In the Riccardi Palace you see the horizontal lines of stones, the windows all in line, the horizontal ledges under the windows, and the long, straight cornice.

Riccardi Palace, Florence

Several famous Renaissance architects followed Brunelleschi. One, named Bramante, made a plan for a great basilica to be built in Rome for the pope. It was to be the largest church in the world, and was to be called St. Peter's. But Bramante died before much work had been done. Several other architects worked on this big building, until it was finally given into the care of the mighty Michelangelo, who was the greatest Renaissance sculptor as well as a great painter, poet, and architect. Michelangelo was an old man, but he pushed the work forward on St. Peter's so that it was almost finished at his death. Michelangelo's plan was to have the church built in the form of a Greek cross, with a magnificent dome over the middle.

Michelangelo made everything about St. Peter's so tremendously large that the building doesn't look as large as it really is. I know that sounds strange. You'd think the bigger a thing was, the bigger it would look. That isn't always so. It depends on the *scale.* If you take a photograph of a tree, you can't tell from the photograph how big the tree is unless there is a man or a dog or a house or *something* near the tree to give you some way of measuring. It is the same with a map: you can't tell whether a town is thirty miles away or three hundred miles unless there is a scale to measure by.

The windows of St. Peter's are about four times as tall as a man. But unless you see a man near them you would naturally think they were about four times as small as they are, because most windows are about as tall as one man.

Long after Michelangelo had died, another architect added a new front to the building, and this cut off the front view of Michelangelo's wonderful dome. This architect also made the church a Latin cross by extending the front. Then still later another man, named Bernini, added two *colonnades,* or rows of columns, to the front. These rows of columns are built around two sides of a great circular open space out in front of the church.

St. Peter's, Rome

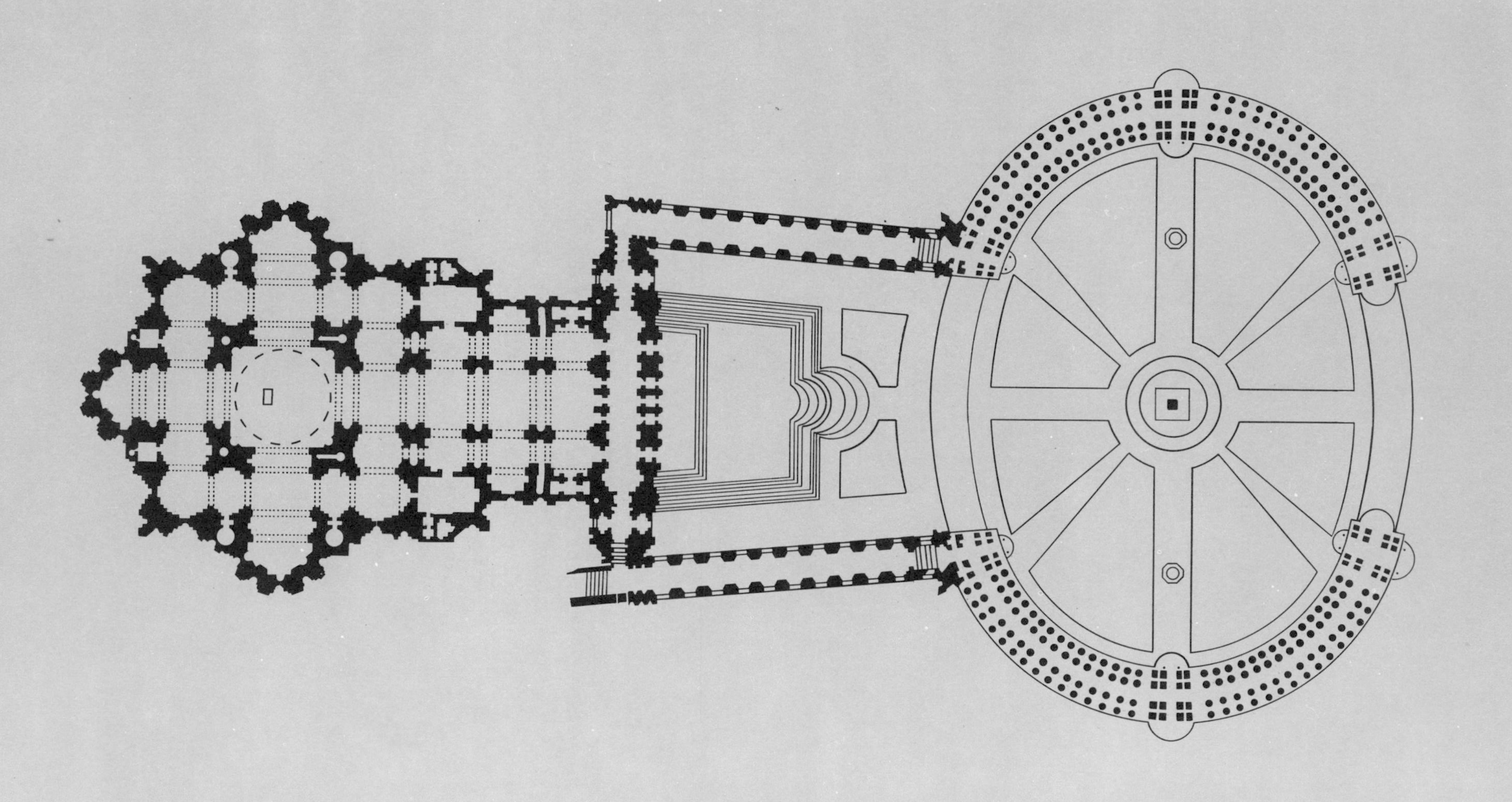

John Hollis—Hollis Associates

The colonnades by Bernini are beautiful, but there isn't anything by which we can judge their size, any more than there is anything by which we can judge the size of the church.

Look at the plan of St. Peter's, showing the building itself and, at the top of the plan, the arrangement of the Bernini colonnades.

Gothic columns were never very much like Roman columns. But the Renaissance architects used the Roman capitals on the columns of their buildings. Sometimes they even pulled down Roman buildings and used the columns for new Renaissance buildings.

There were many famous Renaissance architects in Italy and they have left many famous buildings, but we'll have to skip some of them to tell you about a man named Palladio. Palladio made famous a special use of columns. The columns run from the ground up past two or three stories. This is called the Palladian style. Palladio wrote a book about it which architects in other countries as well as in Italy found useful. The front of St. Peter's shows columns running past two stories.

Renaissance architecture spread from Italy to other countries and has been used until the recent past. All styles of architecture grow out of earlier styles. Renaissance architecture grew by looking backward toward Rome, but its use came at a time when the world was looking forward to greater things. Explorers, scientists, thinkers were showing the way to modern times, though they were getting some of their ideas from studying ancient ways. They were looking backward but moving forward.

Plan of St. Peter's, Rome

English Tudor Architecture

Nearly all the buildings you have read about in this book would make very poor homes. Who would want to live in the Parthenon, or St. Sophia, or the Leaning Tower of Pisa, or Rheims Cathedral? Even the castles and palaces of the Renaissance would be inconvenient for homes unless there were many servants to keep them in order.

Yet from the very earliest times people have had houses to live in. Why haven't these houses been more important in the story of architecture?

One reason is that the houses people live in are not usually built to last as long as a great temple or cathedral. The houses were often built of wood, which gradually decayed. Houses wear out just as shoes or ships do. Old houses are torn down to make room for new ones. Many burn down. So a dwelling as old as a Greek temple would be very hard to find.

Houses that people live in, however, are often more interesting than the great celebrated buildings. For instance, many people like everyday houses of England more than they like the big, handsome, famous public buildings built since the English Gothic cathedrals.

Gothic architecture in England had been slowly changing, until the later Gothic buildings were quite different from the early Gothic buildings. By the time Queen Elizabeth I began to rule, English Gothic architecture had changed so much that it could hardly be called Gothic any more, so it was given a special name. The English rulers at this time belonged to the Tudor family and the architecture was called *Tudor*. Tudor architecture was in between Gothic and Renaissance architecture. Tudor architecture is the most *English* of all English architecture.

Manor houses took the place of the medieval castles. Several of the old manor houses of this Tudor period are still standing. They have big bay windows, sometimes three

British Travel Association Photo

Haddon Hall, a Tudor house in England

stories high. The Tudor windows often had flat tops instead of pointed arch tops like the Gothic, but most of them still had stone tracery in them like the Gothic.

The windows were not arranged in even rows like the windows of the Riccardi Palace in Italy. Whenever a room needed a window, there a window would be put. The chimneys too were put wherever a fireplace was needed, and not just where they would look good from the outside. Often the chimneys were round like columns, instead of being square, and some were twisted like corkscrews.

The Tudor houses were honest architecture. They were built for comfortable and useful homes, not for show with all the beauty on the outside. That is one thing that makes them so pleasant and homelike to look at. They were built of whatever materials could be found in the neighborhood, sometimes stone, sometimes brick, sometimes partly wood and plaster. They seem to fit into the landscape as if they had grown there.

Because the Tudor houses were built for homes, the inside was considered more important than the outside. The outside was not like the outside of Italian Renaissance buildings, which were built mainly for the outside effect.

Indoors on the first floor of a Tudor manor house was the great hall. On the second floor there was often a long gallery or hall running the length of the building. This long gallery connected the rooms of the second story and was often used as a place to hang the family portraits.

In addition to the manor houses, there are many smaller houses of this period still left in England. The first story of these houses is often built of brick and stone. The higher stories have a framework of oak timbers with the spaces between the timbers filled in with brick and plaster. The dark timbers against the white plaster make a very striking effect. They are called *half-timbered* houses.

Many of the old inns and taverns of England are in half-timbered style. Here the stage coaches used to stop. Travelers would find the inns cozy and warm after a long day's journey. Some of these old inns have names like the Fighting Cocks, or the Fox and the Hounds, the Six Bells, the Dolphin, the Feathers, or the Eagle and Child.

Two small half-timbered houses have become very famous. One was the home of the Shakespeare family, and in it William Shakespeare was born. The other was the home of Anne Hathaway, the woman Shakespeare married.

British Travel Association Photo

above: The Rows, half-timbered buildings in Chester, England

below: The half-timbered home in which William Shakespeare was born

British Travel Association Photo

French Renaissance Architecture

You have heard of a fireproof building. But have you ever heard of a fireproof animal? A little animal that looks like a lizard and is called a salamander was—long ago—thought to be fireproof. The people of the sixteenth century thought that if they put a salamander in the fire the salamander wouldn't mind it a bit. The hotter the fire, the more he'd like it. They used to call asbestos cloth—which is fireproof —"salamander's skin."

In those days of the sixteenth century there reigned in France a king named Francis I whose badge was a salamander. Francis I also used a capital letter F as a badge. The salamander and the letter F were like trademarks. Francis I had them put on all the many buildings he built during his reign. He was a powerful monarch with plenty of money to spend and his delight was to spend the money on the works of the best painters, goldsmiths, sculptors, and architects. Many of the painters, sculptors, and goldsmiths were Italians who came to work for Francis I. Most of the architects were Frenchmen.

The buildings of these French Renaissance architects were different from the Italian Renaissance buildings. Most of the French Renaissance buildings were still Gothic in shape. The lines ran vertically up from the ground as they did in the Gothic style. You remember the horizontal lines of some of the Italian Renaissance buildings. This difference was because the Renaissance in France changed from Gothic little by little, while in Italy the Renaissance was not a slow change, but a sudden break from the Gothic.

In Italy many of the Renaissance buildings were churches. In France there were already plenty of fine Gothic churches. Most of the French Renaissance buildings, therefore, were palaces and castles, called *chateaus*.

So many of these chateaus were built along the Loire River in France that the valley of this river is known as the Chateau Country.

A very famous chateau still stands at Blois in the Chateau Country. Parts of the Chateau of Blois were built in the Gothic style before the Renaissance reached France, but one whole section was built by Francis I in the Renaissance

Chateau Blois, France

French Embassy Press and Information Division, New York

style. This section is called the Wing of Francis I. There is a spiral staircase attached to the outside wall of the building in an open tower—something like a fire escape. The staircase tower is stone and marble, like the rest of the building. On the staircase are carved the salamanders and the letter F of Francis I. The salamanders are royal salamanders and each has a crown above him. Little flames of fire seem to be flying all around the salamanders. These trademarks of Francis I appear on other parts of the building, also. The building is still Gothic enough to have Gothic gargoyles on the staircase and roof.

If you should walk down the staircase at the Chateau of Blois and someone else started to walk up at the same time, you two would meet on the stairs. But there is another staircase in France on which persons going down never meet persons going up at the same time. This staircase is in the central tower of a large chateau at Chambord.

The Chateau of Chambord is a huge castle, partly fortified and once protected by a moat or ditch of water. It has towers, steep roofs, tall chimneys, and thick stone walls. With its towers and chimneys pointing toward the sky, it really looks more Gothic than Renaissance.

The interesting staircase is in the tallest tower and works the way it does because there are two sets of steps that corkscrew up the tower together, one set above the other. The Statue of Liberty in New York has an iron staircase inside it built in the same way as the stone staircase at Chambord.

Stairway of the Chateau Blois, France

Photo Air France

French Embassy Press and Information Division, New York

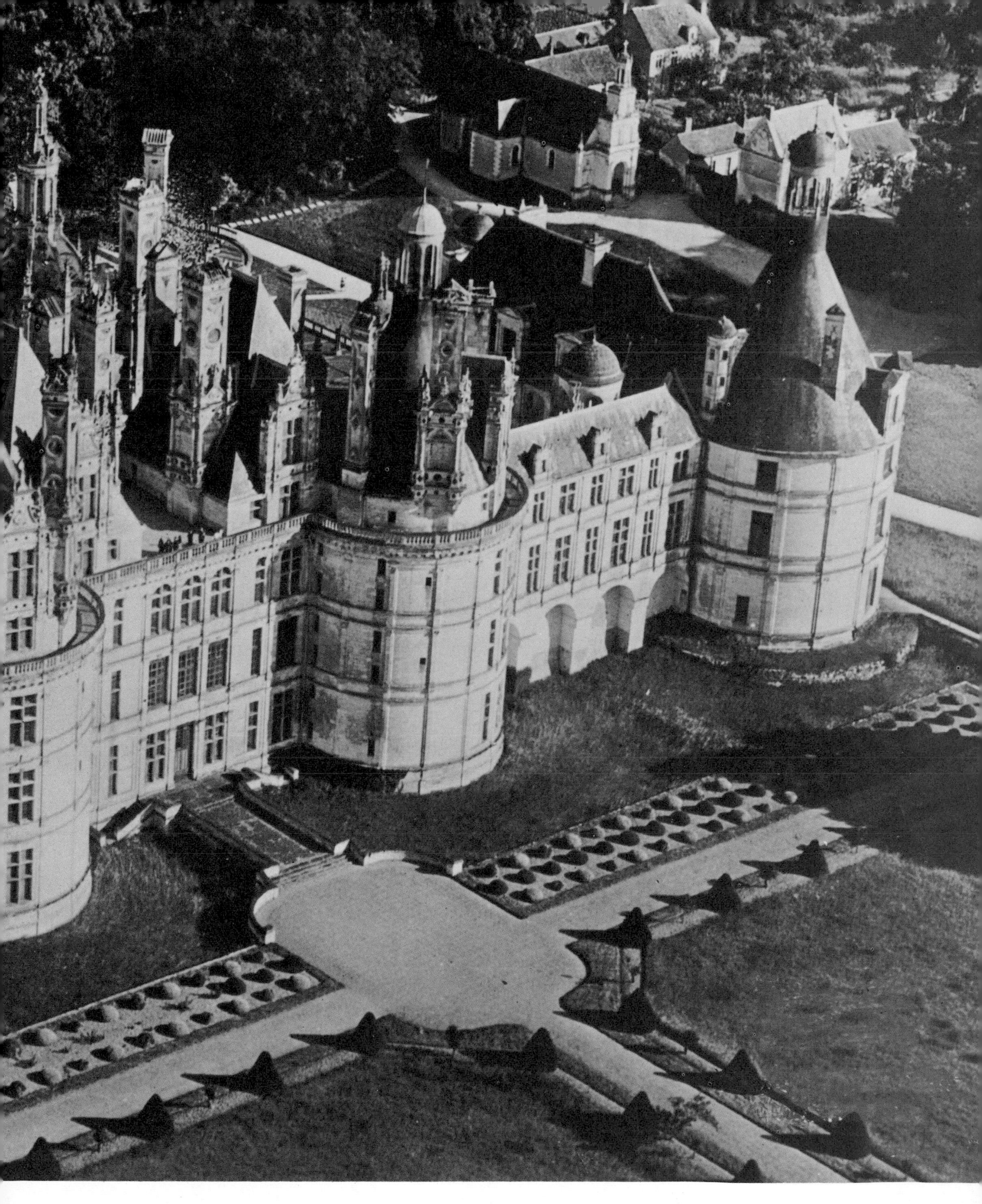

Chateau Chambord, France

French Embassy Press and Information Division, New York

Trans World Airlines, Inc.

Francis I liked to stay at Chambord when he wanted a change from city life. He liked to stay at Blois, too. But he liked best of all the palace of Fontainbleau, which is noted for its beautiful gardens, terraces, and lakes, and for its rich interiors. The outsides of the palace buildings aren't as interesting as Chambord and Blois, so we'll hurry on to still another palace of Francis I. This is the Louvre in Paris.

The Louvre is now the biggest art gallery in the world, but it wasn't built as an art gallery. It was built by kings of France for their use as a palace.

The Louvre is so big—one gallery in it is a quarter of a mile long—that it takes hours and hours just to walk all through it. Of course it wasn't built all at one time. Francis I built part of it. Then other kings added other parts. It wasn't finished until late in the nineteenth century. So the Louvre is a good building to study for a complete history of Renaissance architecture in France, from the earliest to the latest styles.

The Louvre is so big that a photograph doesn't do it justice. In a photograph you can see only one part of it at a time and as each main part looks quite different from its other parts, you really have to be in Paris and see it for yourself to get a good view of it.

Two of the most important of the many architects of the Louvre were Pierre Lescot (Less-koh) and Claude Perrault (Pair-oh). Lescot was the architect for Francis I. Perrault worked a century later than Lescot. Perrault did the famous east façade with its long row of coupled Corinthian columns. A strange fact is that Perrault was the king's doctor, not an architect at all, but he managed to make a very good job of the east façade of the Louvre.

above left: Chateau Fontainbleau, France

below left: The Louvre and Tuileries, Paris

Historical Pictures Service, Chicago

French Embassy Press and Information Division, New York

The Louvre was used as the kings' palace until the French Revolution. Then the king was beheaded and the Louvre was made into a national art gallery. An art gallery is what it has been ever since.

But though Francis I was showy and spent too much money on building, there was a later French king who was even more showy and spent even more money on building even more magnificent palaces. This king was Louis XIV, whose architect built the tremendous palace of Versailles. The palace at Versailles was added to by later kings until France became a republic. It is now owned and cared for by the French Government. Its beautifully laid out grounds add to the magnificence of the palace, but the buildings themselves are monotonous, too much alike, too long and regular. The most famous part is the Hall of Mirrors, a gigantic room with mirrors along the wall. This is where the peace treaty was signed after World War I.

above left: Chateau Versailles

---

below left: The Hall of Mirrors at the Chateau Versailles, France

Historical Pictures Service, Chicago

At Versailles, not very far from the big palace, is a much smaller building called the Petit Trianon. It was built by Louis XV and became the favorite residence of Marie Antoinette, the queen who was beheaded later in the French Revolution.

The French Revolution brings us almost up to the nineteenth century. In the nineteenth century the French erected several buildings that have become famous. One of these is called Hôtel des Invalides, the building that contains the tomb of Napoleon. In it you can see Napoleon's badge or trademark—a capital letter N.

The French Panthéon has a dome that is somewhat similar to the dome of the Invalides, but it has a circle of slim columns around the base. The Panthéon is used as a church and is a shrine to the memory of Saint Genevieve, the patron saint of Paris. It contains the celebrated mural paintings of scenes from the life of Saint Genevieve.

France, and especially Paris, has many other handsome buildings, such as the Madeleine, the Arc de Triomphe, L'Orangerie, the Eiffel Tower, and the Opéra. But we don't have room here to discuss them.

Trans World Airlines, Inc.

above: The French Panthéon, or Church of St. Genevieve, Paris

opposite: Hôtel des Invalides, Paris

Baroque Architecture

The architects of Italy, after about two hundred years of building Renaissance buildings, seemed to get tired of obeying all the rules for building beautiful Renaissance buildings. The rules "cramped their style." In the strict Renaissance architecture almost every part of the building had to be based on some idea from the ancient Romans. The new kind of architecture grew out of the Renaissance architecture, but it tried to break the rules. It was called Baroque architecture. I can't tell you for sure how the word "Baroque" came to be used, but it may have come from a Portuguese word for a badly shaped pearl!

Baroque architecture has been punished by being held up as a bad example ever since. It has really been punished too much, for some Baroque buildings are very fine and very beautiful. The worst Baroque buildings are terrible. They broke too many rules. But the best Baroque buildings are not bad at all. They broke just enough rules to be interesting.

Buildings in the Baroque style are generally very well planned. They fit the place where they are built. They seem to go well with the scenery around them. The trouble with them is that they are too crowded with decoration. They are covered, inside and out, with strange-looking columns and statues and scrolls and twists and fancy marble slabs. They make you think of a very, very fancy birthday cake with icing frills and curlicues all over it.

This Baroque architecture began in Italy. It became the chief architecture of the seventeenth century in that country. And in Italy stands one of the most beautiful of all Baroque buildings. It is a church built beside the Grand Canal in Venice. This church was built for a very special reason. That frightful disease called the plague had killed about a third of all the people in Venice. Sixty thousand people had died. Then the plague stopped. The people who were left alive were so thankful for being spared that they built the beautiful Baroque church as a monument of thanksgiving. They named it Santa Maria della Salute, which means Saint Mary of Good Health. It is pronounced like this: San'tah Ma-ree'ah del'lah Sah-lou'tay.

Santa Maria della Salute is in the shape of an octagon. It has a big dome over the central part and a small dome over the chancel. The buttresses for the dome are shaped like rolls of ribbon.

Santa Maria della Salute, Venice

This fancy Baroque architecture spread all over Italy and into Spain and Portugal. In Spain a few of the Baroque churches are so crowded with decoration that they are really very ugly. Other Spanish Baroque buildings are quite beautiful, although they would be ugly in a country where the sunlight wasn't so bright. The brighter the light, the more decoration a building seems to be able to stand.

Now that we have reached Spain, we come to the people who used Baroque architecture all over the world. In the Roman Catholic Church a body of men like the monks of the Middle Ages was formed to spread the Catholic religion. The men who belonged to this body were called Jesuits. The Jesuits built churches wherever they went, and usually they built their churches in the Baroque style.

In this seventeenth century, the kingdom of Spain was very powerful. The Spaniards had gone exploring. They had taken, in the name of their king, most of South America and a great deal of North America, too. Wherever the Spanish explorers went, the Jesuits soon followed, preaching Christianity to the Indians, founding schools, and building churches. Soon there were more Baroque churches in the Americas than in all of Spain.

These Jesuit churches were so well built that most of them are still standing in spite of earthquakes, revolutions, and neglect. You can imagine what a hard job the Jesuits had. First they had to learn the Indian language or teach the Indians Spanish. They had to show the Indians how to build the stone buildings, often in very hot countries. Yet before the buildings could be built, the land had to be cleared and the stones dug out of the quarries.

The great cathedral at Mexico City doesn't look much like the Santa Maria della Salute. But it, too, is Baroque in style. Baroque architecture also was used in Germany. Some of it came to France, but very little was ever used in England. If you will remember the seventeenth century, Spain and Portugal and their colonies, and Italy and Germany, you will have in your mind the time and places where this very fancy Baroque style was most used.

American Airlines

Night view of the Cathedral and federal buildings in Mexico City

English Renaissance Architecture

About three hundred years ago in England an architect named Inigo Jones went to study architecture in Italy. He saw the Italian Renaissance buildings there. He studied the old Roman buildings, and when he got back to England he began designing Renaissance buildings. They were new to Englishmen, and suddenly everyone wanted a Renaissance building.

Renaissance architecture was late in reaching England, but when it finally did get there, nothing else would do.

Soon a great palace for the king, called the Palace of Whitehall, was designed in the Renaissance style. But the only part of the design that was built was the banqueting hall. This was Inigo Jones's best-known piece of architecture. The Banqueting Hall of Whitehall became a famous building. It looks something like the Petit Trianon at Versailles. It was the first of many English buildings based on the Roman and Italian designs.

The Banqueting Hall looks like a building with two stories, but there is only one story inside—just one big room with a balcony around the walls.

The Banqueting Hall is, however, a beautiful building both inside and out. Notice the Roman columns and the rusticated stonework at the street level, just like the Italian Renaissance buildings. The Banqueting Hall is still called by that name, although it was used as a chapel for many years and finally was turned into a museum.

The next great architect in England after Inigo Jones wasn't an architect at all. At least, not at first. He was an astronomer and a college professor named Sir Christopher Wren.

Sir Christopher Wren became famous as an architect because of a fire. In 1666 a building in London caught fire. The fire spread to other buildings and could not be stopped. Soon a large part of London was burning down. It was one of the biggest fires in the history of the world. Besides London Bridge and thousands of other buildings, over fifty churches were burned. The biggest of these was old St. Paul's Cathedral. Sir Christopher Wren was given the job of making new designs for St. Paul's and for all the other churches.

Sir Christopher thought Gothic was a poor kind of architecture. He liked the Renaissance style, so he built the new St. Paul's Cathedral as a Renaissance building.

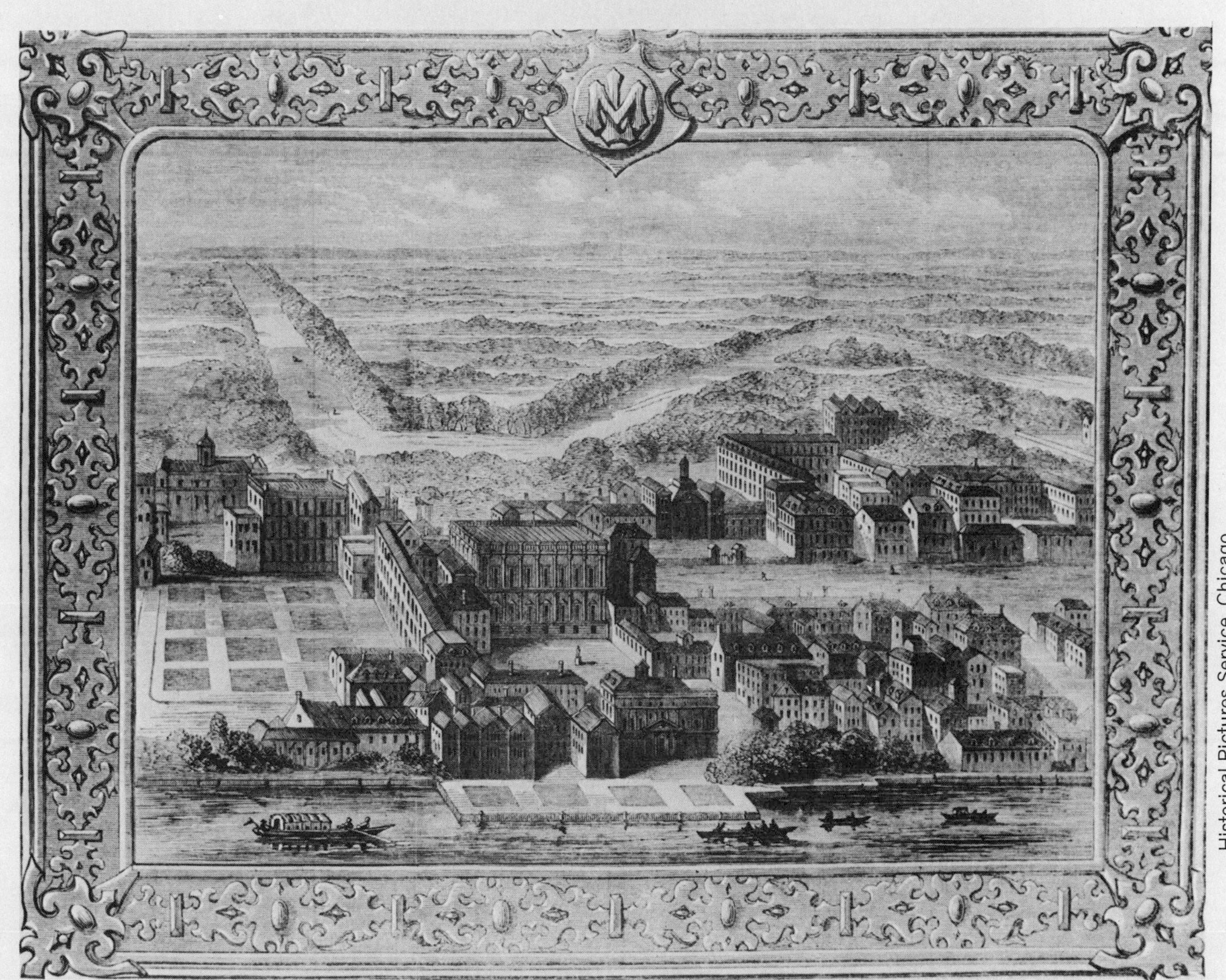

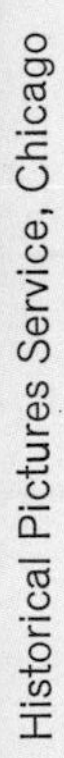

Plan of Whitehall, London. The Banqueting Hall is the large square building in the center of the picture.

British Travel Association Photo

Like the Gothic cathedrals, St. Paul's is in the form of a cross. Over the crossing Sir Christopher erected a very large dome with a stone lantern on top. It is a three-in-one dome—an outside dome, an inside dome for a ceiling, and a brick dome between the other two. This brick dome between the other two was made to hold up the heavy stone lantern.

The outside of St. Paul's has two orders of columns, one above the other. This makes St. Paul's height easier to judge than St. Peter's in Rome, because the two orders of columns give a better scale to judge the height by than the one order of huge columns on St. Peter's.

Unfortunately, St. Paul's wasn't very carefully built. The walls were filled with poor materials and the building, in time, became unsafe. Several years ago it was closed while workmen strengthened the foundations and the supports. Now it is again open and strong enough not to collapse.

Sir Christopher Wren himself is buried in St. Paul's. On his tomb, in Latin, is carved, "If you would see my monument, look around you." St. Paul's is indeed his monument, a great landmark of London and the largest cathedral in England.

As for Sir Christopher Wren's other churches, no two of the more than fifty are alike. Some are noted for the outside design, many for their beautiful interiors, and many more for their graceful steeples. In fact Sir Christopher Wren is famous for his Renaissance steeples. People liked them so well that even in the American colonies churches were built with steeples that look like his designs.

Books were now published giving the rules and designs for Renaissance architecture and many buildings were put up from designs and descriptions in these books. Palladio's book on architecture was translated into English and was used by architects in both England and America.

Renaissance architecture was used in England for many years after Sir Christopher Wren's death. Under the kings George I, George II, and George III English Renaissance architecture had reached a style all its own. This is called the *Georgian* style. I'll tell you more about the Georgian style when we discuss American architecture.

American Airlines

Trans World Airlines, Inc.

above left: Night view of the dome of St. Paul's Cathedral, London

below left: St. Paul's Cathedral, London

right: Christopher Wren Church, Sandwich, Massachusetts

Architecture in America

If you had to go to a wild, unexplored land and live there the rest of your life, what kind of house would you build? Probably you would build a log cabin if you had an axe and could find plenty of trees. But if you had never heard of a log cabin, the chances are you would build some other kind of shelter that you had heard of—a cave perhaps.

The first English settlers who landed in America had never seen a log cabin. What they thought of first were the little huts of the charcoal burners that they had seen in the woods in England. These huts were made of branches and twigs woven together, somewhat as a wicker chair is woven. The early settlers built their shelters like the charcoal huts with steep-pointed thatched roofs—roofs made of straw. When these huts were finished, they must have looked very much like Indian wigwams.

But what about log cabins? Surely the early American settlers used them. Yes, they did use them as soon as Swedish people settled in Delaware. The Swedish had lived in log cabins in Sweden and when they came to America where logs were easy to get, they built log cabins there, too. Then the use of log cabins spread quickly. Log cabins were used by the pioneers and settlers as they pushed westward away from the seacoast, for trees were plentiful.

At least one American log cabin has become famous. It is the one in which Abraham Lincoln was born. Now the whole cabin is kept in Hodgenville, Kentucky, in a big marble building built especially to hold it and protect it.

Some of the early buildings that the settlers from England built were Gothic in style. At Jamestown in Virginia the settlers built a simple little brick Gothic church which has since fallen to pieces. But another small early church called St. Luke's is still standing. St. Luke's has the pointed windows and steep roof of the Gothic style. This seems strange because the Renaissance had reached England some years before America was settled by Englishmen and the Gothic style had gone out of style in England.

Howard E. Gardner, photographer

Log cabin where Abraham Lincoln was born

Commonwealth of Virginia,
Department of Conservation and Economic Development

St. Luke's Church, Virginia

In New England as well as in Virginia some of the early houses were Gothic. They were built of wood and had windows opening at the side on hinges—the way a door opens—with many small panes of glass in each window. They are called *casement* windows. Generally the second story of these houses was a foot or so farther out than the first story, so that there was an overhang in front. Several of these old Gothic houses are still standing.

After awhile books about architecture began to find their way into the American colonies. These books came from England, where Renaissance architecture was in full swing. The books had plans and diagrams or drawings in them which the American carpenters used as guides for making houses. King George was reigning in England—first King George I, then George II, then George III—so the English Renaissance architecture was called *Georgian* architecture. After the first few Gothic buildings, the early American architecture was Georgian too. Now it is called *Georgian Colonial,* or sometimes just *Colonial.*

Most of the Georgian Colonial houses were made of wood in the North and of brick in the South, but in Pennsylvania stone was used. The houses weren't built by regular architects, but by master carpenters who used the books sent from England to guide them.

Besides Georgian Colonial, *Dutch Colonial* was used often, especially by the Dutch settlers in New York. Dutch Colonial houses usually had a roof that sloped down beyond the front of the house to cover the porch.

The Colonial houses were usually plain and simple. They didn't have much decoration like Baroque buildings, which is one reason they seem so charming. Most of the decoration was carved in wood on doorways, mantelpieces, stairways, and ceilings. Sometimes there were wooden pilasters or half columns or columns in the Roman style at each side of the door. Often there was a transom window over the front door decorated with carved wooden tracery sometimes in the shape of a fan, and called a *fanlight*.

Many of these old houses of colonial times are still standing. Most of them, of course, are in the eastern states, which were settled first. Some are famous for reasons other than architecture—Mount Vernon, for instance, because it was the home of George Washington. Mount Vernon on the Potomac is visited every year by thousands of people.

Independence Hall in Philadelphia is famous as the building where the American Declaration of Independence was signed. That is how it got its name. It was designed by a lawyer and is a fine example of Georgian Colonial architecture in brick. The tower reminds us of one of Sir Christopher Wren's steeples in London. In Independence Hall is the famous Liberty Bell which rang so hard that it cracked.

The man who wrote the Declaration of Independence was Thomas Jefferson, later President of the United States. You may be surprised to learn that Thomas Jefferson was one of the best architects of his time. Architecture was not his

Virginia Department of Conservation and Economic Development

Chamber of Commerce of Greater Philadelphia

University of Virginia, photographed by Ed Roseberry

above right: Independence Hall, Philadelphia, Pennsylvania

above left: Mt. Vernon, home of George Washington, in Virginia

right: Aerial view of Jefferson's "Academical Village," the University of Virginia

American Airlines

business but his hobby. He was a great believer in old Roman architecture and he designed many buildings that were Roman in style. One of these is Monticello, Jefferson's own home. He also designed the University of Virginia, with the buildings arranged around the sides of a big square lawn or campus. The white columns against the dark red brick of the buildings are very attractive.

Most of Jefferson's work in architecture was done after the Revolution, so it may seem strange that it is called Colonial, for then the country was no longer part of Great Britain's colonies.

Then came a time when almost all buildings were made with Greek details—Greek columns, Greek shapes. An architect named Robert Mills made a Greek façade of columns for the Treasury Building at Washington. Mills also made the first monument to George Washington—a huge Doric column with Washington's statue on top which stands in Baltimore. The largest and most famous of all the Washington monuments is in Washington, D.C. This is a huge obelisk (you remember the Egyptian obelisks like Cleopatra's Needle), which was not finished for many years after it was begun.

But while the United States was being born in the East, what about the western side of America?

In the Southwest and far West most buildings were Spanish. Mexico had been settled by people from Spain. The Jesuit priests built churches in Mexico, Texas, and New Mexico in the Baroque style. These buildings are called *Spanish Colonial* because they were built in Spanish colonies.

---

left: Washington Monument, Washington, D.C.

About the time of the American Revolution some Spanish monks called Franciscans pushed into California from Mexico. The Franciscans built churches and other buildings there. Their settlements were called missions. They were built along the coast, a day's journey apart, on a road called the King's Highway. A mission was very much like a monastery of the Middle Ages. But because the Franciscans had no one to help them but Indians, they built the missions very plainly and solidly.

Each mission had a church connected by cloisters with other buildings around a courtyard. The buildings usually were made of sun-dried brick, or *adobe.*

This *Mission* style and the Spanish Colonial style were suited to the warm climate of California and the Southwest. In California many of the old missions may still be seen, some in ruins, some carefully preserved.

Another kind of Spanish Colonial architecture grew out of the architecture of the Indians. The Indians of the Southwest—of Arizona and New Mexico—had houses built of adobe. They were really apartment houses, because they had rooms for many families. They were called *pueblos.* Pueblos had flat roofs because there was so little rain. They were often several stories high and had ladders outside so one could get from one story to another.

The Spanish colonists who settled in New Mexico copied this pueblo style from the Indians. Houses in pueblo style always have flat roofs that are on logs whose ends stick out from the top of the walls. The very old Governor's Palace in Santa Fe is built in this pueblo style, although it is only one story high.

New Orleans, settled by the French, introduced from France an architecture with long French windows and iron balconies.

So you see that America in its early days used many different kinds of architecture: log cabins, Gothic Colonial, Georgian Colonial, Dutch Colonial, Spanish Mission, Spanish Indian (pueblo), French Colonial.

American Airlines

Mission at Carmel, California

Washington, D.C.

Every country has a head—a chief ruler, a president, a king, a prime minister, or a dictator. And where the chief ruler makes his headquarters is usually the capital city. "Capital" comes from a word meaning head.

After the American Revolution the new republic of the United States had to have a capital. After trying out both New York and Philadelphia, it was decided to build an entirely new city as a new capital for the new nation.

A place on the Potomac River was chosen, a place of fields and forests. It was named Washington. Frenchmen had helped the Americans in the Revolution and now a Frenchman helped them with the new city. He was Major L'Enfant (Lahn-fanh), who drew a plan for Washington with wide avenues and streets and parks. With L'Enfant's plans to go by, the new city was started. But Washington wasn't much of a city at first—just a few houses in the woods, with "streets" of mud connecting them.

A *capital city* of course needs a *capitol building*. You might think both the city and the building would be spelled alike. But capital spelled with "al" means the city, and capitol spelled with "ol" means the building. A competition was held to find the best design for a capitol. Many good designs were submitted. The one chosen was by Dr. William Thornton. Both George Washington and Thomas Jefferson said they liked the Thornton design very much, and so the Capitol was begun.

If there was to be a capitol, there certainly ought to be a special house for the President. So a president's house was begun the same year as the Capitol. For the first twenty years or so the President's House was always called just that—the President's House. But suddenly the name changed and became the White House. Do you know why?

above left: The White House, Washington, D.C.

below left: Night view of the Capitol Dome, Washington, D.C.

It was because of a fire. Some British soldiers who attacked Washington in the War of 1812 burned both the new Capitol and the President's House. After the fire the President's House still had the walls standing, but the stones were blackened and scorched. The building was repaired and the walls painted white to hide the fire stains, and since then the President's House has been called the White House.

The Capitol had not been finished when it was burned. It too was rebuilt after the fire, but it wasn't finished for years and years. At first this Capitol had a low flat dome over the central part. Then this central part was outgrown and an addition was built on each end of the old building. These new ends are called *wings*—the Senate wing at one end and the wing for the House of Representatives at the other. When the new wings were added a larger dome was designed for the center. During the Civil War, President Lincoln kept work going on this dome even though workmen were scarce. He felt that the dome stood for the Union of the States and that people on the Northern side would be encouraged by seeing this dome growing day by day.

The new dome is almost as big across as the dome of St. Peter's in Rome. It was made of a new building material—not of wood or brick or stone, but iron. To keep iron from rusting, it must be kept painted. Imagine how many buckets of paint forty-three thousand pounds of paint would make. That is more than twenty-one tons, but that's the quantity of paint it takes each time the dome of the Capitol is painted!

One room in the Capitol is called Statuary Hall. That is where each of the states is invited to put two statues of famous men from that state. A whisper can be heard way across Statuary Hall if you whisper from a certain spot that's marked by a metal star in the floor. Strange to say, the star was not put there for the whisper, but to show where the desk of John Quincy Adams used to stand when he was a member of Congress after being President.

The whisper is heard across the room because the waves of sound from that spot all are reflected off the walls and ceiling and meet at another spot on the other side of the room.

The Capitol is full of interesting things. One of these is a subway or underground railroad. The trains are pulled by electric engines and they run from the Capitol to the Library of Congress and to the Senate Office Building and the House Office Building. These three buildings aren't very far away, but the subway trains save the members of Congress time in getting back and forth.

The more you see of the Capitol, the more seems to be left to see. It has often been called the most stately government building in the world. It is important in architecture for another reason, also. It has been such a good building for a capitol that many of the state capitols have been made to look something like it, only smaller. The cornerstone was laid by the first President.

There are many other splendid buildings in Washington. One of these is the Lincoln Memorial. The Lincoln Memorial is built in the Greek style and yet differently. It is Greek and yet it is American. That is because it uses the old Greek forms of columns and other details, but uses them in a new way to fit the kind of building it is. You will notice it has no pediment, or triangular space, above the columns as a Greek temple has.

Washington is one of the most magnificent cities in the world, and is one of the few capital cities planned as a capital before it was even begun as a city.

overleaf, left: Statue of Abraham Lincoln in the Lincoln Memorial, Washington, D.C.

overleaf, right: The Lincoln Memorial, Washington, D.C.

American Airlines
American Airlines

right: A simple beam bridge

below right: The Landwasser Viaduct, an arch bridge in Switzerland

below left: The Crown Point Bridge over Lake Champlain, New York, is a beautiful modern truss bridge.

John Hollis—Hollis Associates

Courtesy of New York State Office of Regional Development.

Swiss National Tourist Office

City of Chicago

right: The Chicago Skyway Toll Bridge, a cantilever bridge

Bridges of the World—Yesterday and Today

In this chapter I'd like to tell you about bridges. There aren't as many different kinds as you might think. Really there are only five kinds of bridges.

The first one is the *simple beam* bridge. A log across a stream is the simplest kind of simple beam bridge.

The second kind is the *arch.* A rainbow would make a beautiful arch bridge, if you could walk across it. There are some beautiful arch bridges in China.

The third kind is the *suspension* bridge. A wild grapevine stem that hangs from one tree to another is a good suspension bridge—for a monkey.

The fourth kind is the *cantilever* bridge (pronounced canta-leaver). A cantilever is a simple beam supported at one end, something like a diving board. Often the bridge has a cantilever coming from both banks of a stream and meeting in the middle.

The fifth kind is the *truss* bridge. A truss bridge has beams strengthened by a stiff framework of different parts fastened together. The framework may either rise above the roadway of the bridge or be beneath it. The frame of a bicycle is something like a truss. Cantilever bridges are often built with trusses. Most truss bridges are built of wood or iron or steel.

These are the five kinds of bridges. What about *pontoon* bridges? Pontoon bridges are just simple beam bridges with the beams resting on boats instead of on posts or piers.

The earliest bridges were beam bridges. Xerxes, a great king of Persia, built a pontoon bridge across the Hellespont when he came to fight the Greeks in 480 B.C.

Strange to say, the Greeks, who could build a perfect building like the Parthenon, were not bridge builders. They traveled by boat more than by road, so they didn't need many bridges. Then too, most of the rivers of Greece are small enough to be crossed without a bridge.

New York Convention and Visitors Bureau

The Brooklyn Bridge, the first suspension bridge built in the New York area

French Embassy Press and Information Division, New York

Pont du Gard near Nîmes, France—a Roman aqueduct with a road on the first level and a canal on the top level

That brings us back to the Romans, the greatest bridge builders until modern times. All roads led to Rome, and the roads had many bridges. Not only in Italy but in Spain and France, in England and in Austria, the fine Roman bridges helped the traveler to get where he wanted to go. Many Roman bridges are still standing and are still in use after two thousand years of service. Some were of wood, and of course they disappeared long ago, but most of them were built of stones so well fitted together that often no mortar was needed.

The biggest Roman bridges were not meant to carry people, however. They were bridges to carry water. When people in ancient Greece needed water they had to carry the water in jars from a stream or well or else use the water right at the stream. But in a Roman city many of the houses had running water and there were also public bath houses where Romans could bathe in beautiful indoor swimming pools full of fresh, clear water. All this water was brought to town by long *aqueducts*, stone bridges with a trough on top. These aqueducts were built across country for miles from the mountain streams to the city.

When an aqueduct came to a valley it didn't go dipping down into the valley and then up on the other side. It went straight across—as a very high bridge indeed. The Romans couldn't make water pipes very well and if the aqueducts had gone down hill and then up again, the water would have spilled out at the bottom of the dip. The best-known aqueduct is now the famous ruin called the Pont du Gard over the river Gard near Nîmes in France.

Swiss National Tourist Office, New York

The Salginatobel Bridge near Schiers in the Prätigau, Switzerland, is a modern arch bridge designed by Robert Maillart.

After the fall of the Roman Empire, bridge building had a fall too. For years and years during the Dark Ages very few bridges were built. Then in the twelfth century A.D. a strange thing happened. Bridges throughout Europe were placed under the care of priests, as they had been in ancient Rome. The priests this time, however, were Christian priests. They formed a society called the Brothers of the Bridge.

At first the Brothers of the Bridge just kept little inns at river crossings, where travelers might stop. But soon they built their own bridges at these places. Often the Brothers made the roadway over the bridge so narrow at the middle of the bridge that only one horseman could cross at a time. This was to make it hard for robbers and soldiers to dash across and attack travelers. Of course such bridges weren't much good for wagons, either. Many of these bridges were strongly fortified with huge stone towers at each end, so that they could stop robber bands or even armies from crossing.

Probably the most famous bridge of the Middle Ages was the old London Bridge over the river Thames. There were houses built on it, some of them four and five stories high, but its foundations weren't very solid, so it was always needing repairs. Parts of it even fell down at various times. At that, it lasted, with many repairs, from 1209 to 1831, when it was torn down to make way for the new London Bridge.

As you know, after the Middle Ages came the Renaissance, when many famous bridges were built. I'd like to tell you about some of them if I had more space—about the most photographed bridge in the world, the Bridge of Sighs in Venice, and about the Ponte Vecchio in Florence, and about the oldest bridge in Paris, which is still called the Pont Neuf or the New Bridge, and about the Pont Royal and the Pont Marie, also in Paris. All these are stone bridges.

Modern bridge building began with the railroads, about 1830. At that time iron bridges were built. Then came steel bridges, and finally concrete and reinforced concrete bridges. Reinforced concrete bridges have iron bars inside the concrete to make them stronger. Many handsome reinforced concrete bridges have been built in recent years. Most of them are arch bridges—sometimes with one arch and sometimes with many. In the United States they are the favorite road bridges.

The iron and steel bridges are often truss bridges. In fact, truss bridges are quite new.

Some of the earliest bridges in Asia and South America were suspension bridges. These were hung from cables of rope or vine and were pretty shaky. Some of them are still in use. They are really quite strong in spite of being so shaky.

Modern suspension bridges are hung from steel cables. Most of them are very large and cost millions of dollars to build. One of the most famous is the Brooklyn Bridge over the East River in New York. Bigger ones have been built since, but this grandfather of modern suspension bridges is still considered one of the finest to look at.

All bridges aren't beautiful, of course, but there are probably fewer ugly bridges than anything else we build; and even ugly bridges usually have an interesting story, if you can find out what it is. One of the ugliest bridges is in Barnstable, England. It has many arches, each one a different size. The size was not planned by an architect, but was determined by the amount of money every citizen donated.

M. E. Warren, Photography, Annapolis, Maryland

right: The Chesapeake Bay Bridge, which connects the eastern and western shores of Maryland, is a suspension bridge nearly four and a half miles long.

Scrapers of the Sky

Very tall buildings, as you know, are called skyscrapers. They are an American invention. Most cities around the world now have skyscrapers. In New York City they are especially exciting to see. From a distance the New York City skyscrapers look like fantastic towers, dream buildings, almost unbelievable.

Gothic cathedrals have tall towers and lofty spires, but compared with the tall skyscraper, the Gothic cathedrals do not look high at all. It is truly amazing that men can build so far above the ground!

It takes a very short time to build a skyscraper. It took hundreds of years, you remember, to build the Gothic cathedrals, but the tallest early skyscraper built—the Empire State Building in New York City—took less than one year to build. And yet it is more than a quarter of a mile high!

Very deep and secure foundations must be laid for modern skyscrapers, and the buildings rise in the air according to schedule. Each steel girder, each sheet of glass, each piece of stone, each section of pipe, is brought to the building site at just the right time. If the wrong piece arrived first, it couldn't be used at once. It would be in the way and would block traffic in the street. The whole building would have to wait. So the materials are hoisted into place at once, instead of being piled up on the ground to wait their turn.

Skyscrapers must be made differently from other kinds of buildings, and it wasn't possible to build them at all until an engineer in Chicago named William Le Baron Jenney solved the main problem involved. In the 1880's Jenney found a way of using steel as the framework of a building.

Each story of the early skyscrapers was a kind of steel cage, and the outside walls were fastened onto the cage. The walls didn't help at all to hold up the building. The

American Airlines

The New York Convention and Visitors Bureau

left: New York Skyscrapers and Statue of Liberty

right: Night view of the Empire State Building

steel cages did all the holding up. The walls were like the walls of a tent—they protected the inside from the weather, but did not help support the weight.

Two other problems in building skyscrapers were solved at about the same time that Jenney solved the framework problem. The engineers found a way of protecting the steel framework against the effects of fire which might otherwise bend it out of shape. They also perfected the elevator, without which tall buildings would be completely useless because people can't walk up and down a dozen flights of stairs, to say nothing of fifty! The first elevators were not as efficient as the ones used today. Now there are locals and expresses so that the top stories can be reached quickly without stopping at each floor all the way up; many elevators are arranged so that a passenger never has to wait for one for more than a minute!

The first skyscrapers were built in the last years of the nineteenth century. These early skyscrapers were shaped like tall shoe boxes standing on end. After many of these box buildings were built, people found that they cut off light from the street below and from the buildings next to them. So some cities made rules that said skyscrapers had to be narrower at the top than at the bottom.

The lower part of a skyscraper, for instance, might cover an entire city block. But when the building had risen a certain number of stories, the stories above had to be set back so the building would not cut off the light. These rules made the later skyscrapers look quite different from the older ones. Today the rules have changed but most cities have laws that require a certain amount of open space to be left on all sides of a skyscraper.

The architects who designed the older skyscrapers had tried to follow the style of some architecture of the past. Some of the early skyscrapers had Greek columns at the base, although the columns carried no weight and weren't used for anything except show. Some had huge cornices at the top that were copied from the Renaissance buildings, but were just as useless and false as the columns. The outsides of these skyscrapers were "fake," and fake architecture can never be very beautiful. Later architects, as we will see, had very different ideas of how skyscrapers should look.

In Chicago an architect named Louis Sullivan went into partnership with an engineer named Dankmar Adler.

Buffalo Chamber of Commerce

The Guaranty Building, Buffalo, New York

Sullivan and Adler combined their talents to show Chicago and the world a new direction in city architecture. They built the first modern skyscrapers in America and the world. The clean, vertical lines of their first two skyscrapers —the Wainwright Building in St. Louis, Missouri, and the Guaranty Building in Buffalo, New York—set the style for buildings that are now going up daily almost everywhere. Many buildings in Chicago were built by the firm of Sullivan and Adler. Not all are skyscrapers, but all showed the beginning of the break from the past.

The stone-faced Auditorium Building on Chicago's Michigan Avenue housed a hotel, an auditorium, and offices. The Adler and Sullivan firm had offices in the tower of the building for many years. The auditorium is the most

Historical Pictures Service

Hedrich-Blessing Photograph

important part of the building, and the most wonderful thing about it is the *acoustical* qualities which Adler gave it. Acoustics is the science of sound control. Good acoustical qualities in a theater make it possible for the audience to hear clearly what is being said even though no microphones are used. Sullivan designed the building itself with its beautiful ornamented interior.

One of the last buildings designed by Sullivan now houses the Carson, Pirie, Scott & Company department store in Chicago. It is a combination of the simplicity that Sullivan felt was necessary in modern architecture and the delicate ornamentation that he loved.

Architects after Sullivan tried to give their buildings shapes that were beautiful in themselves and didn't need the type of decoration that Sullivan often used. The hundreds of windows of a skyscraper are no longer just holes in the wall. They are used to add to the beauty of a building or to *be* the beauty of a building. In some skyscrapers the windows look like stripes running from the ground to the top. They seem to carry the eye upward as do the lines of a Gothic cathedral. In others the windows are arranged in rows that make stripes across the building instead of up and down. In still others, the windows *are* the building—just a continuous sheet of glass!

Some skyscrapers are used as offices where people work. Some are used as apartments where people live. Skyscrapers have to be useful and have to make money after they are built, for it costs millions of dollars to build one. Their rooms are rented for offices, hotels, apartments, shops, or factories. In many skyscrapers there are banks, restaurants, stores, or even theaters on the first floor.

Skyscrapers seem wonderful at a distance, they seem wonderful near at hand, and the more one learns about them, the more wonderful they seem. If you've never seen a skyscraper, it will give you an idea of how very high they are when I tell you that the mail chutes have to be made in a special way to slow up the letters dropping down from the top, for otherwise the letters would go so fast they would be scorched!

above left: The Auditorium Theater Building, Chicago

---

below left: Carson, Pirie, Scott & Company, Louis Sullivan

Hedrich-Blessing Photograph

Taliesin West, Arizona; Frank Lloyd Wright, Architect.

Hedrich-Blessing Photograph

Kaufman residence, Bear Run, Pennsylvania. Frank Lloyd Wright, Architect. Nicknamed Falling Water.

Frank Lloyd Wright

Many men have contributed their ideas to modern architecture—ideas for the design and construction of private homes, churches, skyscrapers, and even ideas for complete city planning.

One of the best-known architects, Frank Lloyd Wright, worked with the firm of Adler and Sullivan. Wright was Sullivan's student and he completely changed architecture with his original ideas. While working with Adler and Sullivan, he used his own time to design many private homes and to develop his own ideas.

Wright believed that buildings should be beautiful in themselves and that they should fit into their surroundings. Taliesin (Tally-es-in), one of Wright's homes, is built in the hills of Wisconsin very near the place where he was born. Nature played a very important part in the design of this house with its many rooms, terraces, and overhanging roofs. The same kind of roof sweeps far out over the balconies in the Robie House in Chicago.

Nature and building seem to be part of one another in Wright's winter house near Phoenix, Arizona. This home is called Taliesin West. He used purplish-red stone from the nearby desert area for the walls, and timbers for the roof. The building is surrounded by desert cactus plants and looks as if it belongs there.

One of the most popular homes Wright built is called Falling Water. This house is built in a rocky glen near a waterfall. Local stone was used for the walls and smooth concrete for balconies.

In the construction of his homes Frank Lloyd Wright always tried to use materials that could be found near the building site. The materials and the design were combined to give a feeling of unity to the house and the setting. Wright erected many buildings throughout the United States—homes, churches, office buildings, and other structures. In Tokyo, Japan, he built a hotel. There Wright had the problem of building in an earthquake area. He decided to "float" the hotel on soft earth instead of sinking its

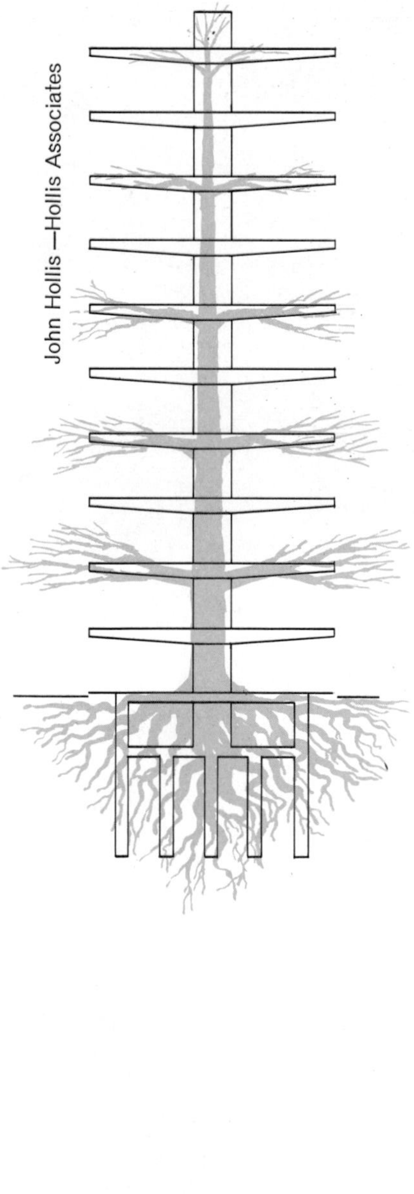

John Hollis—Hollis Associates

foundations to bedrock. He split the building into separate, loosely connected sections that would not crack apart in an earthquake. Each section had its own supports. A few years after the hotel was completed, an earthquake struck Tokyo, and though many buildings in the area of the Imperial Hotel were damaged, the hotel remained standing. This was proof indeed of Frank Lloyd Wright's architectural genius!

Wright believed so strongly that architecture should follow nature that he used one of nature's ideas even in his skyscraper design. The structure of a tree seemed to him a good model to use. A tree has a firm foundation and a central support with horizontal branches spreading from the support. In architecture this is now called *core and cantilever* construction. The core is like the trunk of a tree and floors spread out from the core like branches of a tree. The Johnson Wax Tower, built in 1950 from Wright's design, has a central support, or core, made of concrete and horizontal floors—cantilevers—enclosed in glass.

Wright wanted to build a mile-high building in Chicago using this type of construction, but engineers and architects in that city didn't think it was possible and he never had the chance to try it out. Recently a British engineer has designed a building *two* miles high, using four cores instead of just one. Maybe someday someone will build buildings that tall and prove that it can be done. Think of buildings one or two miles high!

Core and cantilever construction was used in Marina City in Chicago. These twin apartment buildings on the Chicago River are sixty stories high. In Milwaukee, Wisconsin, the city has built a core and cantilever apartment building for housing elderly people.

In New York City Wright used concrete in a plastic, sculptural way in the design of a spiral-shaped building, the Guggenheim Museum. This art museum building seems to wind upward and becomes wider at the top. On the inside, the spiral gently winds downward to the first floor. Paintings hung around the walls are lighted by a skylight that forms the ceiling of the great circular room. There are also open spaces in the walls that help to add light. The visitor sees the paintings as he walks down the curving ramp.

Diagram showing the similarities between the structure of a tree and that of a core and cantilever building.

Photographic Department, S. C. Johnson & Son, Inc.

American Airlines

American Airlines

Hedrich-Blessing Photograph

above: Marina City, Chicago. Bertrand Goldberg, Architect.

---

top left: Johnson Wax Tower, Racine, Wisconsin

---

middle left: Interior view of the Guggenheim Museum showing skylight

---

bottom left: Exterior view of the Guggenheim Museum

Steel and Glass—Walter Gropius and Mies van der Rohe

Have you ever seen a house all made of steel and glass? A steel and glass house has no ancestors. But most styles of architecture do have ancestors, long lines of ancestors.

Just as the Roman style developed from the Greek, the Romanesque style from the Roman, and the Gothic style from the Romanesque, so until recently most new styles have grown out of past styles of architecture.

This modern use of past styles seemed right as long as the modern buildings had the same uses as the buildings of the past. But many modern buildings have entirely new uses not even conceived of by the architects of past styles. And so it seems to architects today that these buildings should be free from the influence of the past. It wouldn't make sense to design a modern electric powerhouse in the Gothic style when there is no connection between a powerhouse and any building built when Gothic architecture was in its glory; nor would it make sense to have Roman columns on a gasoline station when the Romans had never even heard of gasoline!

Photograph courtesy of Walter Gropius

Shoe Last Factory, 1910-1911. Walter Gropius with Adolph Meyer. (The Fagus Works)

While Adler, Sullivan, and Wright were working in Chicago, European architects were laying a foundation for modern architecture. The works of Frank Lloyd Wright had been published in Europe in 1910, and were a tremendous influence on the modern architecture of Europe. Among those who were influenced by Wright were the German architects Walter Gropius and Ludwig Mies van der Rohe.

Gropius was the pupil of an already famous architect in Germany named Peter Behrens. The first building designed by Gropius was a shoe factory, the Fagus Works, built in 1911. In this building Gropius used a steel frame and glass walls with no supports at the corners, so that the glass met at the corners. This had never been done before. Gropius used glass again in the group of buildings that made up the Bauhaus in Dessau, Germany, a school

Photograph courtesy of Walter Gropius

Bauhaus, Dessau, 1926. Walter Gropius.

of architecture and design that was completed in 1926. Gropius was director of this school, and taught modern design to the students there; he also taught them the importance of architects exchanging their ideas with each other and cooperating in their work.

Gropius left Germany and, in 1938, became Chairman of the Department of Architecture at Harvard University in Cambridge, Massachusetts. He built the Graduate Center there and, working with other architects, has designed many buildings for the United States and other countries.

The work of Ludwig Mies van der Rohe was acclaimed by people the world over when they saw his design for the German Pavilion for an exposition in Spain. This building was very beautiful but very simple. It had a low, plain travertine base and floor-to-ceiling walls of glass and green marble, covered by a flat rectangular roof that was supported by eight cross-shaped steel columns. The pavilion opened into two courts with pools lined in black glass. The thing that made this building important was that there were no doors in it—one space flowed into the next and connected with the space outside. It was a new kind of architecture.

During the next few years, Mies designed and built many buildings in Europe. He erected a house in Czechoslovakia in 1930 that had an inside wall made of onyx, pronounced on'-icks, and another of striped ebony. Onyx

is a soft-colored stone with a milky look, something like marble. Ebony is a very dark, nearly black, hard wood. Very little color was used in the building itself, but the trees that are near the house can be seen through the glass walls and give the building as many changing colors as there are in all the changing seasons.

In 1938, Mies was asked to become head of the School of Architecture at Chicago's Armour Institute, which is now called the Illinois Institute of Technology (I.I.T.). He accepted the offer, and also designed a whole new I.I.T. campus which spread over eight city blocks. Mies used a steel framework for each of his buildings and brick and glass for the outside walls. The buildings are far enough apart so that their design can be seen easily.

Many people feel that a house Mies built on the Fox River in Illinois is the most perfect example there is of pure simplicity in architecture. He built the Farnsworth House with walls of glass. Eight steel columns support the roof and the floor and also raise the building several feet off the ground—just in case the Fox River overflows! The interior of the house is one large open room with an enclosed area in the middle that contains the kitchen, bathrooms, and a fireplace. On our cover is a picture of this house in the woods.

In 1919 Mies made a sketch on paper of a glass office building; the following year he made a sketch of another glass building intended to be thirty stories high. These two sketches became the basis for all steel and glass skyscrapers built today. Steel and concrete were the basic, or fundamental, parts of the buildings and glass was the covering.

above left: Barcelona Pavilion exterior showing walls and pool

below left: Interior of Barcelona Pavilion looking toward sculpture court. The wall at the left is bottle green glass, the one at the back in the sculpture court is green tinian marble, and the wall in the middle of the room is onyx. The floor is travertine.

Hedrich-Blessing Photograph

Joseph E. Seagram & Sons, Inc.

above: The Seagram Building

---

top right: 860-880-900-910 N. Lake Shore Drive, Chicago. Ludwig Mies van der Rohe, Architect.

Mies designed the first steel and glass skyscrapers ever built. Two of his four apartment buildings—860-880 N. Lake Shore Drive in Chicago, have a framework of steel with clear glass sides. The ground floor of each building is enclosed in glass and set back. The columns, which are covered with black steel plate, come down the faces of the buildings to a terrace. The 900-910 buildings are of reinforced concrete, but look very much like the steel and glass pair. Light and shadow on the glass sides of the buildings change the way they look at different times of the day. Sometimes the clouds are reflected in the glass, sometimes a sunset, and sometimes the sides look nearly black.

In 1958, Mies designed and built the Seagram Building in New York. This tall steel and glass skyscraper, set in the middle of Manhattan, is raised on columns like the buildings in Chicago. It is set back from the street so that it can be seen clearly by anyone passing by. On the inside of the building Mies used beautiful marble, stainless steel, and of course, glass. Philip Johnson worked with Mies on this building. Many buildings have been designed by Mies van der Rohe and because architects have imitated his work so often many buildings by others look as if he had designed them.

Sculptured Concrete— Le Corbusier

During the period in which the first modern architects did most of their building, new things also were being done in painting. Artists were experimenting in brand new abstract forms of art. Today many people still consider these kinds of art daring and modern. Imagine what people thought about them when they were first being done! The changes in art influenced many architects. A French architect named Le Corbusier was a painter as well as an architect and was most interested in the shapes used by the *cubist* painters—cubes, squares, circles, cones, triangles, and rectangles.

Le Corbusier's Savoye House in France is a white cube on stilts with continuous bands of windows and a flat roof to be used as a garden. He built many houses but this is his finest one.

As Mies used steel, Le Corbusier used concrete. Concrete is made by mixing sand, gravel, and cement with water. In the beginning of the twentieth century, concrete came to be used in a different way than it had been used before. It

French Government Tourist Office, Chicago

French Embassy Press and Information Division, New York

was combined with steel bars to make *reinforced concrete.* The concrete supports the weight and the steel prevents it from cracking.

After World War II, Le Corbusier designed a fifteen-story apartment house in Marseilles, France. Two of the floors are for shopping areas. The apartments extend the entire width of the building and have living rooms two stories high opening out onto balconies. The building was made from very rough concrete with pieces of stone or shells showing and impressions from the molds into which the concrete had been poured. It is supported by massive columns. The walls separating the balconies are painted in bright colors and on the roof is a large recreation area with many interesting forms made from concrete. There is a nursery school, pool, restaurant, benches, a movie screen of concrete, and even a cinder running track! This roof is really a work of sculpture in concrete.

A chapel by Le Corbusier in Ronchamp, France, made from curved concrete, looks much like the buildings in Greece that he admired so much. The rough walls are white stucco and windows of different sizes, some with stained glass, are dotted over the walls. Light comes into the chapel at different angles and in different colors through all these little windows.

Among Le Corbusier's greatest contributions to the twentieth century were his ideas for city planning. In 1922 he planned a city to house three million inhabitants. In the center of the city were tall buildings for offices and space for parks, and extending out from the center were low apartment houses and more parks and courts, so that pedestrians could wander anywhere. The apartment buildings were on stilts and had shopping levels above the street and public plazas on their roofs.

Le Corbusier wrote many books, pamphlets, articles, and papers about his new and exciting ideas, and many city planners today are using them.

above left: Le Corbusier's apartment building in Marseilles, "Radiant City"

---

below left: Chapel at Ronchamp, Notre Dame du Haut, by Le Corbusier

Architecture Today

Many other men made contributions to the beginning of modern architecture. One of the most important of these came from the northern part of Europe—Scandinavia. Norway, Denmark, Sweden, and Finland are Scandinavian countries. We often see Scandinavian design in furniture, flatware, and glassware, but not so widely known are Scandinavian architectural designs. Eliel Saarinen, a Finnish architect, came to the United States in 1923 and built and headed an art school in Michigan. He also erected other buildings in the United States and many of them were designed with the help of his son, Eero. Among these were the Summer Music Pavilion at the Berkshire Music Center in Massachusetts; the Tabernacle Church of Christ in Columbus, Indiana; and the Crow Island School in Winnetka, Illinois.

Sullivan, Wright, Gropius, Mies van der Rohe, Le Corbusier, and Saarinen all contributed much to what we call modern architecture. Through their buildings, speeches, writings, and teaching they have inspired many other men to design buildings in the architectural styles that were created by them.

Today's architects are using the ideas of these men and also ideas of their own. Groups of architects and engineers, rather than individuals, often work on the design and construction of buildings. This kind of cooperation and exchange of ideas and experience, you remember, was encouraged by Walter Gropius at the Bauhaus.

The United Nations Secretariat Building was designed by a group of architects from different countries. The large glass building overlooking the East River in Manhattan is the result of the combined efforts of this group of men. It seems very fitting, doesn't it, that men from many nations should have worked together to build such a building as this? It is, as it was meant to be, a true expression of the spirit of the United Nations.

The new Lincoln Center for the Performing Arts in New York also was designed by a group of architects working as a team. The Lincoln Center buildings, to be used for

1965, Lincoln Center for the Performing Arts (Bob Serating Photo)

A model of Lincoln Center for the Performing Arts.

plays, symphonies, operas, and other productions, are arranged around a central plaza. Another team of men designed the Y-shaped building in Paris that houses the offices of UNESCO, the United Nations Educational, Scientific and Cultural Organization.

One large architectural firm that employs many architects and engineers who work either in teams or by themselves is Skidmore, Owings & Merrill. Many of their buildings look very much like those of Mies van der Rohe. Lever House, a glass skyscraper with a broad base and a slender tower built in Manhattan in 1952, was one of the first glass skyscrapers designed by this architectural firm. They also designed a low, graceful, glass office building set in open country for the Connecticut General Life Insurance Company; the Inland Steel Building, one of the first steel and glass office buldings built in the crowded loop area of Chicago; and the 100-story John Hancock Center—designed to contain offices, shops, parking, and apartments—that is now being built in Chicago.

New buildings are being designed and built every day all over the world. Architects are using steel, concrete, reinforced concrete, glass, marble, stone, wood, and brick in these buildings. Some are very unusual and not everyone likes all of them, just as not everyone likes the same kinds

Lever Brothers Company, New York

Hedrich-Blessing Photograph

Hedrich-Blessing Photograph

opposite left: Lever House

opposite right: Model of John Hancock Center, Chicago

left: Inland Steel Company building, Chicago. Skidmore, Owings & Merrill, Architects.

of food, weather, music, or books. There isn't room here to mention all the buildings designed and built by the men who were the pioneers of modern architecture, and nowhere near enough room to tell you about all the buildings that are being built by the men who are following these pioneers. The last ones I would like to mention are the latest in the long line of architects that began with the pyramid-builders of ancient Egypt. It is interesting to see how modern architecture is developing.

Marcel Breuer designed a monastery church in Minnesota that uses plain materials. It has an entry made of a gigantic concrete slab from which are hung the original bells cast in 1879. The interior of the church has a brick floor, concrete walls, and oak pews. The materials he used are beautifully plain and inside one's eye is immediately drawn to the white granite altar.

St. Paul's Lutheran Church in Sarasota, Florida, designed by Victor Lundy, comes closer to a revival of the Gothic feeling than do the designs of most other modern architects. Lundy has used laminated wood beautifully in his soaring roof that curves down almost to the ground from a very high central peak. A very different kind of church architecture has been created in the aluminum and glass Air Force Chapel in Colorado, designed by Walter A. Netsch, Jr., one of the architects at Skidmore, Owings & Merrill in Chicago.

The shell form we see so often in nature has also been used in modern architecture. The construction of thin, curved shell forms of reinforced concrete is difficult but it can be very beautiful. Pier Luigi Nervi, an engineer, designed a sports stadium for the 1960 Olympics in Rome. Nervi made a beautiful reinforced concrete shell dome 300 feet in diameter, more than twice the size of the gigantic dome of St. Peter's Basilica. It is made of pre-cast concrete which is molded, or cast, in a factory and then brought to the construction site and erected.

above left: St. Paul's Lutheran Church. Victor Lundy, Architect.

below left: The Cadet Chapel at the Air Force Academy in Colorado has seventeen spires rising 150 feet upward.

Courtesy of Ernest C. French, D.D., Pastor

Santa Fe Railway. Photography by R. Collins Bradley.

Italian State Tourist Office-Enit, Chicago

MAS—Art Reference Bureau

Many schools have been designed, and in one—the great University City of Mexico—brightly colored mosaics were used to decorate the library building. The Chicago campus of the University of Illinois, called the Chicago Circle Campus, is now being built in what was once a very crowded area. Land was cleared to provide space for the much needed city university. A twenty-eight story administration building, a library, several lecture halls and buildings for classrooms will be reached by raised walks that will also connect the buildings on the campus with outside transportation facilities.

Eduardo Torroja designed a racetrack in Spain with reinforced concrete canopies that stretch out more than forty feet over the seating section! The canopies of this Hippodrome provide shade and protection from the weather for the spectators. They are a series of connected arches supported by columns at the outside wall of the building.

An engineer named Robert Maillart has built very beautiful reinforced concrete bridges in his home country of Switzerland. His longest bridge spans about 300 feet over a steep gorge.

Airport terminals are necessary in our modern world and many have been built. The concrete TWA Terminal Building at the Kennedy International Airport in New York and the Dulles International Airport Terminal in Washington, D.C., were both designed by Eero Saarinen. The design of the Lambert-St. Louis Airport Terminal won an award for the architect, Minoru Yamasaki.

Cities are growing so fast these days, and spreading out so far from the centers, that it is becoming more and more difficult for people who live on the edge of one of them to reach the city shopping areas. This problem has been solved in many areas by the development of large shopping centers that contain a variety of stores and have plenty of parking space. It is possible to drive to one of these shopping centers, park your car, cash a check at a currency exchange or bank, buy groceries, purchase department store goods, do your laundry at a laundromat, have lunch at a restaurant, and buy bread at a bakery, all without leaving a very small

American Airlines

The mural-covered library at the University of Mexico, Mexico City.

above left: Roma-Palazzetto dello Sport (Small sport building) designed for the 1960 Olympics in Rome.

below left: The Hippodrome in Madrid, Spain, designed by Eduardo Torroja.

Chicago Circle Campus, University of Illinois. Skidmore, Owings & Merrill, Architects.

Hedrich-Blessing Photograph

TWA Terminal Building

Photo by Ezra Stoller Associates, Trans World Airlines, Inc.

Old Orchard Shopping Center, Skokie, Illinois. Loebl, Schlossmen & Bennett, Architects.

Hedrich-Blessing Photograph

area! The walks in these shopping centers are often covered, so that anyone walking from one store to another is protected from the weather. One of the most beautiful shopping centers, and one of the first to be built, is Old Orchard, on the outskirts of Chicago.

City planning, of course, is of vital interest to all of us. Totally new cities, like Canberra, the capital of Australia; Chandigarh, the capital of the Punjab state in India; and Brasilia, the capital of Brazil, have been planned for and built in the wilderness. The capital city of the United States, Washington, also was created from scratch. Most city planners, however, have to plan around already existing buildings. This makes the problem of good planning much more difficult than it would be in an open area. *Urban renewal* is a common phrase in city planning today. Slum buildings are demolished by the city's department of urban renewal. Usually the city buys the property, tries to find other locations for the residents and businesses, and then clears the land. The cleared land is sold to developers who build apartments, office buildings, shopping centers, and factories on it. Lake Meadows, a private project in Chicago, is an example of such redevelopment.

Much still remains to be done, however, to make our cities livable because they have become overcrowded and the problem of automobile traffic has become a serious one. Our present cities, laid out during the horse and buggy era, were not designed to cope with the many thousands of automobiles which today clog our streets and endanger human life. People who were able to have moved to the city suburbs where they can live in agreeable surroundings. Our cities are antiquated and need to be replanned for present-day living. Overall city planning is required, not the piecemeal kind which is being practiced in all of our cities today.

It will be interesting for you to watch the ideas in architecture and city planning grow as you grow. Someday you yourself perhaps may help to clear away the slums of the world and design new homes, apartments, and office buildings to take their places.

INDEX: Young People's Story of Architecture, Gothic to Modern

Abbey churches/**21**
Abencerrages, Hall of the, Alhambra, Granada/**36**
"Academical Village," University of Virginia/**80**
Acoustics/**101**
Adams, John Quincy/**87**
ADLER, DANKMAR/**98-101, 103**
Adobe/**82**
Africa/**37**
Agra, India/**40, 41**
Air Force Chapel, Colorado/**118, 119**
Airport terminals/**121, 122**
Alhambra, Granada/**36, 38, 39**
Ali Baba/**35**
Allah/**37**
America, Architecture in/**76-89, 94-110, 114-123**
Amiens Cathedral, France/**19**
Antwerp Cathedral, Belgium/**27, 29**
Antwerp Town Hall, Belgium/**27**
Aqueducts/**92, 93**
Arabesques/**36, 37**
Arabia/**37**
Arabian Nights, The/35
Arabs/**37, 39**
Arcades/**32**
Arc de Triomphe, Paris/**67**
Arch bridges/**90, 91, 93, 94**
Arches, Pointed/**11,13**
Arches, Ribbed/**13**
Arches, Round/**11**
Arizona/**82,102, 103**
Armour Institute, Chicago, Ill./**109**
Asia Minor/**11**
Auditorium Building, Chicago, Ill./**99-101**
Australia/**123**
Bagdad/**37**
Baltimore, Maryland/**81**
Banqueting Hall, Whitehall, London/**72, 73**
Barcelona Pavilion, Spain/**107, 108**
Barnstable, England/**94**
Baroque architecture/**68-71, 81**
Barrel vaults/**10, 13**
Bauhaus, Dessau, Germany/**106, 107**
Beam bridges/**90, 91**
Behrens, Peter/**106**
Belgium, Architecture in/**27-29**
Berkshire Music Center, Mass./**114**
BERNINI/**49, 51**
Blois, Chateau of, France/**56-59**
Blue Mosque, Istanbul/**34**
BRAMANTE/**49**
Brasilia, Brazil/**123**
BREUER, MARCEL/**119**
Bridge of Sighs, Venice/**94**
Bridges/**90-95, 121**
Brooklyn Bridge, New York/**91, 94**
Brothers of the Bridge/**93**
BRUNELLESCHI/**42-45**
Brussels Town Hall, Belgium/**28**
Buffalo, New York/**99**
Burgos Cathedral, Spain/**30, 31**
Buttresses/**11-13, 15**
Buttresses, Flying/**12, 13, 15**
Cadet Chapel, Air Force Academy, Colorado/**118, 119**
Cairo, Egypt/**37**
California/**82, 83**
Cambridge, Massachusetts/**107**
Canberra, Australia/**123**
Canterbury Cathedral, England/**24, 25**
Cantilever bridges/**90, 91**
Capital cities/**85**
Capitol buildings/**85**
Capitol, Washington, D.C./**84-87**
Carmel, California/**83**
Carson, Pirie, Scott & Co., Chicago, Ill./**9, 100, 101**
Casement windows/**78**
Cathedral, Mexico City/**70, 71**
Cathedral of Chartres, France/**17**
Cathedral of Notre Dame, Paris/**14, 15, 17**
Cathedral of St. Mark, Venice/**32**
Cathedrals/**14-32, 42-45, 70-72, 74, 75**
Catholic religion/**70**
Centering/**10, 11**
Chambord, Chateau of, France/**59-61, 63**
Chandigarh, India/**123**
Chapel at Ronchamp, France/**112, 113**
Chapel of Henry VII, Westminster Abbey/**24**
Chartres Cathedral, France/**17**
Chateau Blois, France/**56-59**
Chateau Chambord, France/**59-61**
Chateau country/**56**
Chateau Fontainbleau, France/**62, 63**
Chateaus/**56-65**
Chateau Versailles, France/**64, 65**
Chesapeake Bay Bridge, Maryland/**95**
Chester, England/**55**
Chicago Circle Campus, University of Illinois/**121, 122**
Chicago, Illinois/**4, 9, 90, 97-101, 103-105, 109, 110, 115-117, 121-123**
Chicago River/**4, 104**
Chicago Skyway Toll Bridge, Illinois/**90**
China/**91**
Christian Renaissance architecture/**40**
Christopher Wren Church, Sandwich, Mass./**75**
Churches/**14-32, 42-45, 48-51, 67-72, 74-77, 81, 82, 114, 118, 119**
Church of St. Genevieve, Paris/**67**
City Planning/**113, 123**
Civil War, United States/**86**
Cloth Hall, Ypres, Belgium/**29**
Cologne Cathedral, Germany/**14, 26, 27**
Colonnades/**49**
Colonial architecture/**78-82**
Columbus, Indiana/**114**
Columns, Corinthian/**63**
Columns, Doric/**81**
Columns, Gothic/**49, 51**
Columns, Palladian/**51**
Connecticut General Life Insurance Co. Building/**115**
Constantinople/**39**
Cordova mosque, Spain/**38, 39**

Core and cantilever construction/**104**
Corinthian columns/**63**
Country cathedrals, England/**20-25**
Cornices/**47**
Court of the Lions, Alhambra, Granada/**38, 39**
Cross, Greek/**49, 68**
Crossing/**17**
Cross, Latin/**17, 49**
Crow Island School, Winnetka, Ill./**114**
Crown Point Bridge, Lake Champlain, New York/**90**
Crusades/**11**
Cubists/**111**
Cupola/**43**
Decorated Gothic architecture/**24**
Declaration of Independence/**79**
Delaware/**76**
Dessau, Germany/**106, 107**
Doge's Palace, Venice/**32, 33**
Dome of the Invalides, Paris/**66, 67**
Domes/**35-37, 42-44, 66-68, 75, 86**
Doorways/**14, 17, 19, 21**
Doric columns/**81**
Dormer windows/**29**
Dulles International Airport Terminal, Washington, D.C./**121**
Duomo, Florence, Italy/**43, 44**
Durham Cathedral, England/**21, 22**
Dutch Colonial architecture/**78**
Dutch settlers, New York/**78**
Early English Gothic architecture/**22**
East River, New York City/**94, 114**
Egypt/**37**
Eiffel Tower, Paris/**67**
Elevators/**98**
Elizabeth I/**52**
Empire State Building, New York City/**97**
England, Architecture in/**20-25, 52-55, 72, 75, 93**
English country cathedrals/**20-25**
English Renaissance architecture/**72-75**
English settlers, America/**76**
English Tudor architecture/**24, 52-55**
Facades/**17**
Fagus Works, Germany/**106**
Faith, Giralda Tower, Seville/**39**
Falling Water, Bear Run, Pennsylvania/**102, 103**
Fanlights/**79**
Farnsworth House, Ill./**109**
Florence, Italy/**42-44, 46, 47, 94**
Flying buttresses/**12, 13, 15**
Fontainbleau, Chateau, France/**62, 63**
Fox River, Ill./**109**
France, Architecture in/**14-19, 56-67, 92, 93, 111-113**
Francis I/**56, 59, 63, 65**
Franciscan monks/**82**
French Colonial architecture/**82**
French Gothic cathedrals/**14-19**
French Panthéon, Paris/**67**
French Renaissance architecture/**56-67**
French Revolution/**65, 67**
Gard River, France/**92, 93**
George I/**75, 78**
George II/**75, 78**
George III/**75, 78**
Georgian architecture/**75, 78**
Georgian Colonial architecture/**78, 79**
German Pavilion, Spain/**107, 108**
Germany, Architecture in/**26, 27, 70, 106, 107**
GHIBERTI/**42, 43**
Gibraltar, Strait of/**37**
Giralda Tower, Seville/**39, 40**
Glass, Stained/**16, 17, 19**
Glass walls/**11,12, 17**
Goldberg, Bertrand/**105**
Gothic architecture/**10-33, 76, 78**
Gothic cathedrals/**14-32**
Gothic columns/**49, 51**
Goths/**10**
Governor's Palace, Santa Fe, New Mexico/**82**
Graduate Center, Harvard University/**107**
Granada, Spain/**36, 38, 39**
Grand Canal, Venice/**68**
Grand Place, Town Hall, Brussels, Belgium/**28**
Greek cross/**49, 68**
GROPIUS, WALTER/**106, 107**
Guaranty Building, Buffalo, N.Y./**99**
Guggenheim Museum, New York City/**104, 105**
Guildhalls/**29**
Guilds/**14, 29**
Haddon Hall, England/**53**
Half-timbered houses/**54, 55**
Hall of Mirrors, Versailles, France/**64, 65**
Hall of the Abencerrages, Alhambra, Granada/**36**
Harvard University, Cambridge, Mass./**107**
Hathaway, Anne/**54**
Hellespont/**91**
Henry VII Chapel, Westminster Abbey/**24**
Hippodrome, Madrid, Spain/**120, 121**
Hodgenville, Kentucky/**76**
House Office Building, Washington, D.C./**87**
Illinois Institute of Technology, Chicago, Ill./**109**
Imperial Hotel, Tokyo, Japan/**103, 104**
Independence Hall, Philadelphia/**79, 80**
India, Architecture in/**40, 41, 123**
Indians, American/**82**
Inland Steel Building, Chicago, Ill./**115, 117**
Inns, English/**54**
Invalides, Dome of the, Paris/**66, 67**
Istanbul, Turkey/**34**
Italian Renaissance architecture/**46-51**
Italy, Architecture in/**32, 33, 42-51, 68, 69, 94, 119, 120**
Jamestown, Virginia/**76**
Japan/**103, 104**
JEFFERSON, THOMAS/**79-81, 85**
Jenney, William LaBaron/**97**
Jesuits/**70, 81**
John Hancock Center, Chicago, Ill./**115, 116**
JOHNSON, PHILIP/**110**
Johnson Wax Tower, Racine, Wis./**104, 105**
JONES, INIGO/**72**
Kaufman residence (Falling Water), Bear Run, Pa./**102, 103**
Kennedy International Airport, New York City/**121**
King's Highway/**82**
Koran/**35, 37**
Lake Champlain, New York/**90**
Lake Meadows, Chicago, Ill./**123**
Lake Michigan/**110**
Lake Shore Drive, Chicago, Ill./**110**

Lambert-St. Louis Airport Terminal/121
Landwasser Viaduct, Switzerland/90
Lantern/43
Latin cross/17, 49
LE CORBUSIER/111-113
L'Enfant, Major Pierre Charles/85
LESCOT, PIERRE/63
Lever House, New York City/115, 116
Liberty Bell/79
Library of Congress, Washington, D.C./87
Lincoln, Abraham/76, 77, 86-89
Lincoln Cathedral, England/24
Lincoln Center for the Performing Arts, New York City/114, 115
Lincoln, Memorial, Washington, D.C./87-89
Loebl, Schlossmen & Bennett/122
Log cabins/76
Loire River, France/56
London Bridge, England/93
London, England/24, 25, 72-75, 93
L'Orangerie, Paris/67
Louis XIV/65
Louis XV/67
Louvre, Paris/62, 63, 65
LUNDY, VICTOR/118, 119
Madeleine, Paris/67
Madrid, Spain/120, 121
MAILLART, ROBERT/93, 121
Manor houses/52-54
Marie Antoinette/67
Marina City, Chicago, Ill./4, 104, 105
Marseilles, France/112, 113
Maryland/94
Mecca, Arabia/37
Mexico, Architecture in/70, 71, 81, 121
Mexico City/70, 71, 121
Michigan Avenue, Chicago, Ill./99
MICHELANGELO/49
MIES VAN DER ROHE, LUDWIG/106-110
MILLS, ROBERT/81
Milwaukee, Wisconsin/104
Minarets/37
Minnesota/119
Mission architecture/82, 83
Modern architecture/97-123
Mohammed/37
Mohammedan architecture/34-41
Mohammedan religion/37
Mohammedan tombs/35,40
Monastaries/20
Monks/20, 82
Monticello, Virginia/81
Moors/31, 39, 40
Mosque of d'Ibn Tonloun, Cairo/37
Mosque of Sultan Ahmed I, Istanbul/34
Mosques/34-39
Mount Vernon, Virginia/79, 80
Muezzins/37
Napoleon/67
Nave/14, 17, 19
NERVI, PIER LUIGI/119
NETSCH, WALTER A., JR./119
New England/78
New Mexico/81, 82
New Orleans, Louisiana/82
New York City/2, 91, 94, 96, 97, 104, 105, 110, 114, 115, 116, 121, 122
Nîmes, France/92, 93
Notre Dame Cathedral, Paris/14, 15, 17
Notre Dame du Haut, Ronchamp, France/112, 113
Obelisks/81
Old Orchard Shopping Center, Skokie, Ill./122, 123
Olympics, 1960, Rome/119, 120
Opéra, Paris/67
Palace of Whitehall, London/72, 73
Palladian columns/51
PALLADIO/51, 75
Panthéon, Paris/67
Paris, France/14-17, 63, 66, 67, 94, 115
Parthenon/19
Perpendicular Gothic architecture/24
PERRAULT, CLAUDE/63
Persia/37, 91
Peterborough Cathedral, England/24
Petit Trianon, France/67
Philadelphia, Pennsylvania/79, 80
Phoenix, Arizona/103
Plague/68
Pointed arches/11, 13
Pont du Gard, Nîmes, France/92, 93
Ponte Vecchio, Florence/94
Pont Marie, Paris/94
Pont Neuf, Paris/94
Pontoon bridges/91
Pont Royal, Paris/94
Portals/19
Portugal/70
Potomac River/79, 85
Prätigau, Switzerland/93
President's House, Washington, D.C./85, 86
Prince Agib/35
Proportion/27
Pueblos/82
Racetrack, Madrid, Spain/120, 121
Racine, Wisconsin,104, 105
"Radiant City," Marseilles, France/112, 113
Reinforced concrete construction/94, 113, 119, 121
Religion, Mohammedan/37
Renaissance architecture/42-51, 56-67, 72-75
Rheims Cathedral, France/18, 19
Ribbed arches/13
Ribbed vaults/11, 12
Riccardi Palace, Florence/46, 47
Robie House, Chicago, Ill./103
Roman architecture/45, 92, 93
Roman bridges/92, 93
Roman Catholic Church/70
Romanesque architecture/10
Rome, Italy/39, 48-57, 119, 120
Romo-Palazzetto dello Sport, Rome/119, 120
Ronchamp, France/112, 113
Rose windows/17
Round arches/11
Rows, The, Chester, England/55
Rusticated stonework/47
SAARINEN, EERO/114, 121
SAARINEN, ELIEL/114
St. Chapelle Church, Paris/16, 17

St. Genevieve, Church of, Paris/**67**
St. Louis, Missouri/**99, 121**
St. Luke's Church, Virginia/**76, 77**
St. Mark's Cathedral, Venice/**32**
St. Paul's Cathedral, London/ **72, 74, 75**
St. Paul's Lutheran Church, Sarasota, Fla./**118, 119**
St. Peter's, Rome/**48-51**
St. Sophia/**39**
Salamanders/**56, 59**
Salginatobel bridge, Switzerland/**93**
Salisbury Cathedral, England/**22, 23**
Sandwich, Massachusetts/**75**
Santa Fe, New Mexico/**82**
Santa Maria della Salute, Venice/**68, 69**
Sarasota, Florida/**119**
Savoye House, France/**111**
Scale/**49**
Scandinavian design/**114**
Schiers, Switzerland/**93**
Seagram Building, New York City/**110**
Senate Office Building, Washington, D.C./**87**
Seville, Spain/**39, 40**
Shakespeare, William/**54, 55**
Shoe Last Factory (Fagus Works), Germany/**106**
Shopping centers/**121-123**
Simple beam bridges/**91**
Sinbad the Sailor/**35**
Singing towers/**29**
Skidmore, Owings & Merrill/**115, 117, 119, 122**
Skokie, Illinois/**122**
Skyscrapers/**97-101**
Spain, Architecture in/**30, 31, 36, 38-40, 70, 107, 108, 120, 121**
Spanish Colonial architecture/**81, 82**
Spanish Indian architecture/**82**
Spanish Mission architecture/**82, 83**
Spiral staircase, Chateau Blois/**59**
Spires/**17, 22**
Sports stadium, Rome/**119, 120**
Stained glass/**16, 17, 19**
Staircases/**59**
Statuary Hall, Capitol, Washington, D.C./**86, 87**
Statue of Liberty/**59, 96**
Steeples/**75**
Strait of Gibraltar/**37**
Subway, Capitol, Washington, D.C./**87**
SULLIVAN, LOUIS/**9, 98-101, 103**
Sultan Ahmed I, Mosque of, Istanbul/**34**
Summer Music Pavilion, Berkshire Music Center, Mass./**114**
Suspension bridges/**91, 94**
Swedish settlers, America/**76**
Switzerland, Architecture in/**90, 93, 121**
Tabernacle Church of Christ, Columbus, Ind./**114**
Taj Mahal, Agra, India/**40, 41**
Taliesin West, Arizona/**102, 103**
Taliesin, Wisconsin/**103**
Taverns, English/**54**
Texas/**81**
Thames River, England/**93**
Thornton, William/**85**
Tokyo, Japan/**103, 104**
Tombs, Mohammedan/**35, 40**
TORROJA, EDUARDO/**120, 121**
Tours, France/**37**
Towers/**14, 17, 21, 24, 29**
Towers, singing/**29**
Town Hall, Antwerp, Belgium/**27**
Town Hall, Brussels, Belgium/**28**
Tracery/**19**
Transepts/**17**
Treasury Building, Washington, D.C./**81**
Truss bridges/**90, 91, 94**
Tudor architecture/**24, 52-55**
Tuileries, Paris, France/**62**
Turkey, Architecture in/**34**
TWA Terminal Building, New York City/**121, 122**
UNESCO Building, Paris, France/**115**
United Nations Secretariat Building/**2, 114**
United States, Architecture in/**76-89, 94-110, 114-123**
University of Illinois, Chicago Circle Campus/**121, 122**
University of Mexico, Mexico City/**121**
University of Virginia/**80, 81**
Urban renewal/**123**
Vaults, Barrel/**10, 13**
Vaults, Ribbed/**11, 12**
Venice, Italy/**32, 33, 68, 94**
Versailles, Chateau, France/**64, 65**
Virginia/**76, 77, 79-81**
Wainwright Building, St. Louis, Mo./**99**
Walls, Glass/**11, 12, 17**
War of 1812/**86**
Washington, D.C./**81, 84-89, 121**
Washington, George/**79-81, 85**
Washington Monument, Baltimore, Md./**81**
Washington Monument, Washington, D.C./**81**
Weather vane, Giralda Tower, Seville/**39**
Wells Cathedral, England/**24**
Westminster Abbey, London/**24, 25**
Wheel windows/**17**
Whitehall, London/**72, 73**
White House, Washington, D.C./**84-86**
Windows, Casement/**78**
Windows, Dormer/**29**
Windows, Rose/**17**
Windows, Tudor/**54**
Windows, Wheel/**17**
Wings/**86**
Winnetka, Ill./**114**
Wisconsin/**103, 104, 105**
World War I/**19, 29, 65**
WREN, SIR CHRISTOPHER/**72, 75**
WRIGHT, FRANK LLOYD/**102-105**
Xerxes/**91**
YAMASAKI, MINORU/**121**
Ypres, Belgium/**29**

Type *Century Expanded*
Typesetter *American Typesetting Corporation*
Printer *The Regensteiner Corporation*